Running Elections
by Roger Morris and David Monks

© SOLACE Enterprises Ltd. 2001

All rights reserved. No part of this publication may be reproduced, stored in a retrieval system, or transmitted, in any form, or by any means, electronic, mechanical, photocopying, recording or otherwise, without prior permission, in writing, from the publisher.

Typeset in Verdana, 10pt

Designed by Ashley Harris, SOLACE Enterprises

Printed and bound in the United Kingdom by
P.W. Design

ABOUT THE AUTHORS

ROGER MORRIS

Roger Morris has been Chief Executive of both the City of Durham (1981-1986) and Northampton Borough Council (since 1986), and has been involved in running elections for over thirty years. He has been President of the Association of District Secretaries (1979-1980) and of SOLACE (1995-1996). He has written widely on local government topics, and is currently a member of the Society's Electoral Matters Panel.

DAVID MONKS

David Monks is Chief Executive of Huntingdonshire District Council, a position he has held since 1995. He has worked for five local authorities and prior to 1995 was Chief Executive of North Warwickshire Borough Council for twelve years. David has been involved in election work throughout his local government career, has been a returning officer for eighteen years and is the current Chairman of the SOLACE Electoral Matters Panel. He served on the Home Office Howarth Working Party on reforming Electoral Procedure, gave evidence to the Home Affairs Select Committee investigating elections, and is a regular speaker and writer on election topics.

March 2001

CONTENTS

		Page
	Introduction	7
1.	The Background to Election Law	9
2.	Electoral Registration	12
3.	Different Kinds of Elections	17
4.	Returning Officers and Deputies	27
5.	Polling Districts and Polling Places	33
6.	Polling Stations	35
7.	Things To Do First for Elections; & Casual Vacancies	38
8.	Insurance	41
9.	Appointing Election Staff	43
10.	Working with Election Agents	46
11.	Handling the Nomination Process	48
12.	The Returning Officer's Role During the Campaign	54
13.	Poll Cards	57
14.	Absent Votes	59
15.	Polling Agents and Tellers	62
16.	Planning the Count	64
17.	On Polling day	69
18.	Conducting the Count	71
19.	When the Election Is Over	76
20.	Election Fees and Staff Payments	78
21.	Election Petitions	80
22.	The Returning Officer's Accounts	82
23.	Local Election Experiments – Pilots	84
24.	Combined Elections	86
25.	Changes of Areas	89
Appendix 1	Further Reading and Sources of Information	92
Appendix 2	Parliamentary Election Timetable	95
Appendix 3	County Election Timetable	96
Appendix 4	Regions for the European Elections	97

INTRODUCTION

Newly appointed Chief Executives who are probably not lawyers (let alone "electoral anoraks")[1] Often ask whether there is something they can read about running elections. Certainly it is not essential to be a lawyer to be a successful returning officer, however, it is worthwhile, to have a working knowledge of electoral law, and it is upon that basis that the authors have prepared this text.

Even so, it is not a publication about election law as such. Rather it is about responsibility for the management of elections. It goes without saying that having properly run, free and fair elections is a cornerstone of democracy in any community. Similarly every chief executive (or indeed anyone else who may be responsible) should recognise that running elections properly and efficiently is a key aspect of job retention and success. The public, your employing authority, and your own staff all need to have confidence in what's happening from their own standpoints.

These pages should help to grow and keep that confidence. They draw input from the SOLACE Enterprises Ltd courses of recent years on running elections, and the authors welcome comments on their relevance, helpfulness, and any omissions. In 25 short chapters we present a series of themes (relating to England and Wales) which you won't find – not like this anyway – in conventional textbooks or encyclopaedias like Parker and Schofield. Moreover, both experienced returning officers and electoral administrators will find the publication useful in checking reference points, particularly for specific provisions in legislation.

Running elections is a very personal, and sometimes lonely, responsibility. Everyone who carries that responsibility needs to think about the issues we present. Our intention is simply to help you to have the confidence then to make your own decisions, as you must, usually within a very unforgiving timetable. There is a very high standard of electoral administration in this country which often makes the whole process appear almost mechanical and routine; but the most experienced returning officer will always be wary, for dangers lurk

---

[1] A phrase coined by George Howarth MP in a Parliamentary debate and quoted in Hansard.

beneath dark electoral waters - they usually turn out to be sharks, not icebergs!

Because references to the Representation of the People Acts and Regulations occur so frequently they are abbreviated to "RPA" or "RPR" appropriately. We have tried to refer to the law as we understand it on 1 March 2001, i.e. following the operation of the Representation of the People Act 2000, the Representation of the People (England and Wales) Regulations 2001, and the Local Elections (Principle Areas) Amendment Rules 2001.

We record our appreciation of the help given in preparing this book by Sandy Bennett and Caroline Wilson on the secretarial and editorial aspects respectively.

Roger Morris
David Monks

CHAPTER 1
THE BACKGROUND TO ELECTION LAW

As one of the oldest or longest-running democracies, elections in the UK go back hundreds of years, and there are echoes of this still on the statute book in relation to Parliament in particular.

The present system is essentially Victorian in construction and tone, with the secret ballot dating back to the Ballot Act 1872 and even earlier legislation. Reform of our voting process is overdue, to reflect the technology, lifestyles and expectations of the early years of the twenty-first century. Nevertheless we may salute a system which served well for several generations, and was so enduring that it survived all that time when so much else was changed – including the scope of the franchise for which the processes were originally devised.

The written procedures and documentation still need to be compared against that original purpose - to be honest, fair, and at once both secret for the individual voter and open to inspection for the confidence of candidates and the electorate at large. It will be much harder to improve the reputation for integrity than it will be to improve the physical act of voting and remove any justification for the use of sealing wax. In fact, of course, much has anyway changed over the years. In the Public Libraries Act 1850, whose sesquicentennial was recently celebrated, voters on whether to adopt the Act had to sign their names on their votes, whereas today we still expect a cross, the traditional mark of the illiterate. In s 2 of the Ballot Act 1872, the returning officer was forbidden to vote, even in secret, yet if a tie resulted he had to give his casting vote, so publicly declaring his preference! (A provision which has now been thankfully repealed, but returning officers can draw lots in the event of a tied result.)

Another historical principle, and one still very important today as part of the safeguards of integrity, or constitutional checks and balances, is contained in the appointment of returning officers. Through statutes and Parliamentary and constitutional procedures, the Crown dissolves and summons Parliaments. A writ – the term still survives here despite its abolition in everyday legal use – is issued as an instruction to officials acting locally to "return" (hence "returning officer") the writ with the name of the elected candidate on it.

That official, however, is not appointed by the Crown, or Parliament, or any Minister, but by the prescribed local authority for all, or a substantial part, of each constituency concerned. Though the returning officer is technically either the county high sheriff or a district chairman or (lord) mayor – see chapter 3 – the official who does all the management and administrative work, styled the "acting returning officer", is appointed by that local authority, which appoints other proper officers similarly for other electoral (and additional) functions. Technically the acting returning officer need not otherwise be an employee of that council, though in practice always is (see chapter 4).

The network of rules about how to run and participate in elections is detailed and, as already stated, now in need of reform, but it has to meet three principal objectives: it has to be clear and fair to administer, and deal with all the likely eventualities; it has to be demonstrably and openly fair to candidates and voters, so that they can scrutinise what takes place and check compliance with the law for themselves; and it has to be secret in terms of voters' choices, yet able to be reviewed by a court if legally challenged.

The rules have also to be considered against that original social and technological background, so different from today's. That may well produce a different verdict from contemporary opinion: those differences may be instructive in checking how proposals for reform would affect the requirements of principle that have been found to serve well in the past.

A problem both in reading and describing election law is its repetitive and convoluted nature. Many rules are all but identical for different sorts of elections, and are set out separately for each in different regulations. There is considerable scope, reform and modernisation apart, for simply rationalising what is there. The past three years alone have seen two new systems of elections added, for the Welsh Assembly and the Greater London authority, and a third, for the European Parliament, remodelled; outside the scope of this book changes for the Scottish and Northern Ireland Assemblies have come about also, and now in 2001 regulations for referendums on directly elected mayors are being introduced. A consolidating Elections Act, simplifying the cumbersome "representation of the people" style, would be a useful step in itself. The authors have argued for such steps to be followed in other places, at the time of preparing this text, without success - but see the reference in the first paragraph of chapter 23 to the 1999 Report of the Home Office Working Party on Electoral Procedures.

The real problem with regulations as they change and modify existing election rules is that they are produced in a "jigsaw" style. Thus, there is never a *de novo* start from a blank sheet of paper to produce a composite set of rules for a particular election when there is substantial change such as the European election of 1999. The existing rules are always modified or replaced to a certain extent and the poor practitioner has to juggle with a number of weighty texts before him to try and see the whole picture. In the European Election Training Project a composite set of rules was produced by a practitioner and printed in one separate document (see section A of chapter 3).

At this stage it is also worth noting that the vast majority of these regulations emanate from the Home Office who, traditionally, in our system of government promote electoral legislation. This has been the situation for very many years but is now changing. Thus the DETR, as part of its modernisation agenda, is promoting regulations dealing with mayoral referendums and these are drafted within that Department; see sections K and L of chapter 3.

The detailed legal rules and regulations are to be found in the standard works like Parker and Schofield. Of course this book can be no substitute for them. It seeks only to provide a general map to intricately constructed territory.

CHAPTER 2
ELCTORAL REGISTRATION

Electoral registration, the compiling and keeping of the electoral register, is a separate function from running actual elections, but is inevitably intertwined with it.

The system is now changing from an essentially Victorian base, involving compiling the register once a year with reference to a fixed base date of 10 October, to a so-called "rolling register", involving continual change. The latter approach better reflects today's rapidly moving society, and was used for the collection of the community charge in the late 1980s and early 1990s.

Nevertheless its introduction is not without technical difficulties. The previous annual electoral register (or "roll") was already variable to a degree: a monthly list of claims to be added meant that the original totals were not immutably final for the year, although claims to be added still had to be referred to the qualifying date of the last 10 October.

The core provisions have hitherto been ss 8-13 of the RPA 1983. In England, district, unitary, metropolitan and London Borough councils (plus the Common Council of the City of London) had to appoint a registration officer under s 8 of the Act; in Wales, every county and county borough had to do so under the same section, as amended. Note that it is specifically the registration officer who is to be the acting returning officer for Parliamentary election purposes under s 28 (1) (a) of the 1983 Act, and that in turn this person will be the local returning officer for European purposes (see chapter 4), so the original appointments are very important. The term "registration officer" is not used, however, in defining the returning officer for local elections in s 35 (1), (1A) and (3) of the RPA 1983, or therefore (since the local returning officer designation is followed) in the definition of "counting officer" for elected mayor referendums (see K in chapter 4).

The duty to "prepare and publish in each year" in s 9 of the RPA 1983 gave the registration officer considerable discretion in how to set about the task, and how far to go in obtaining the responses which local residents are by law obliged to provide. Most would undertake an annual canvass in order to compile the draft register (which had to be published by 28 November), and then respond to further changes so as to enable the formal register to be published no later than 15 February to come into force on 16 February (s 13 (1) of the 1983 Act). The "electors lists" were published as the draft register under the RPR 1986, SI No 1081 para 35. The law has now been substantially recast by the Representation of the People (England and Wales) Regulations 2001 SI No 341.

All peers of the realm were formerly unable to vote at Parliamentary elections, but now hereditary peers who have no House of Lords seat can do so – see the House of Lords Act 1999, s 3 and the Holders of Hereditary Peerages (Extension of the Franchise) (Transitional Provisions) Order 1999, SI No 3322.

Registers for different kinds of elections are combined so far as possible (s 9 (2)), with various letters printed to indicate particular limitations or entitlements. These various letters are as follows, collated from different provisions, for electoral registers in force from 16 February 2001:

"Marking of Names

42
(1) Paragraphs (3) to (7) below specify the marks to appear against a person's name in the register to indicate that he is registered in one or more of the four registers (those of: parliamentary electors; local government electors, relevant citizens of the Union registered as European Parliamentary electors and peers overseas registered as European Parliamentary overseas electors) which are required to be combined.

(2) Where no mark appears against a person's name in the register of electors, this indicates that he is registered in the registers of parliamentary and local government electors.

(3) To indicate that a relevant citizen of the Union is registered only in the register of local government electors, the letter 'G' shall be placed against his name.

(4) To indicate such a citizen is registered in both that register and the register of such citizens registered at European Parliamentary electors, the letter 'K' shall be placed against his name.

(5) To indicate that any other person is registered only in the register of local government electors, the letter 'L' shall be placed against his name.

(6) To indicate that an overseas elector is registered only in the register of parliamentary electors, the letter 'F' shall be placed against his name.

(7) To indicate that a European Parliamentary overseas elector is registered only in the register of such electors, the letter 'E' shall be placed against his name."

The coming into force of the relevant provisions of the RPR 2001, from which para 42 above is taken, replaces the annual register, as referred to above, with a rolling register (and also replaces the absent votes procedures of ss 5-9 of the RPR 1985 – see chapter 14).

Section 9 of the RPR Act 1983 is substituted by para 3 of sch 1 to the RPA 2000, and contains in what becomes s 9 (6) "the duty to take reasonable steps to obtain information required" to perform the duty of maintaining the register.

Section 10 of the 1983 Act (substituted by para 4 of sch 1 to the 2000 Act) requires an annual canvass to be undertaken for updating the electoral register, but moves the qualifying date to 15 October. This formal statutory requirement for an annual canvass was less explicitly required by the previous section 10, which merely referred to having "a house to house or other sufficient inquiry". Following it a revised version of "both registers" must be published by 1 December (or a later date if regulations so prescribe): see s 13 (1) of the RPA Act 1983 as substituted. "Both registers" in fact just refers to Parliamentary and local government elections: as before, both sets of lists must "so far as practicable be combined" (s 9 (5) as substituted).

Sections 13A and 13B added into the 1983 Act deal with ongoing alterations to the register, and the final date for changes effective for any given election (normally close of nominations). This is the equivalent of the former claims procedure; on the previous procedure see the former s 11 to the RPA 1983 and the associated paras 58 – 62 of the RPR 1986, SI No 1081.

Note in relation to draft registers and claims generally the possibilities for hearings (regs 29-32 of RPR 2001): just as there are statutory penalties for failure to supply correct information for inclusion in the electoral register (reg 23 of the RPR 2001), so it is not unknown for people to try and register – perhaps using a name or address of convenience – solely for the purpose of establishing credit references or separating themselves from poor credit records associated with other addresses. Giving false information to such an end is of course an offence.

The detailed requirements for the rolling register are set out in the RPR 2001. These have now revoked almost all of the RPR 1986, SI No 1081 and subsequent applicable amending regulations.

The new 2001 Regulations replace the previous rules of paras 53-56 of the RPR 1986 on the supply of free copies of electoral registers and associated provisions about the sale of registers and supply of data and labels. Reg 47(2), reflecting the gradual change from paper to electronic copies of recent years, sets out "data form" supply as normal unless a printed paper copy is specifically requested. The supply of lists of overseas electors is provided for alongside the main electoral registers.

An MP or MEP is entitled to a free copy of the relevant part of any register – it is to be recognised, of course, throughout this chapter that registration officers work to local authority and not Parliamentary constituency boundaries, so that arrangements are often necessary to provide for correlation.

One free copy of the appropriate register or part must also be supplied free on demand to local councillors, local election candidates (or their agents), registered political parties and parish councils, or in Wales, community councils. Parliamentary candidates or agents can also obtain copies.

The register must also be available for general sale – a requirement not without its controversial side in today's climate of both computer technology and personal security. In data form it will cost £20 plus £1.50 per 1,000 entries (or part thereof), and in printed form £10 plus £5 for each 1,000 entries (or part thereof) (so long as the registration officer has enough copies left to sell – see reg 48 (4)). The former provision about supplying data and labels are not continued, as today's technology has rendered them unnecessary when every registration officer is a "data user". Separate charges are made for the list of overseas electors. (See reg 48, RPR 2001).

Finally it is worth noting the growing practice of registration officers avoiding disenfranchising homeless or itinerant people by allowing them to register at identifiable locations which are not homes in the ordinary sense, like doorways or public areas etc. This concept is called 'notional residence' and, for instance, the homeless person seeking to claim such 'residence' to the electoral returning officer must make a declaration of local connection - see s 7B of RPA 1983 and reg 41 of RPR 2001. There will be some obvious difficulties with such addresses, but they are perhaps preferable to loss of a potential right to vote, and how to register in such cases is ultimately a matter for local policy within the scope of the law. For further discussion see *RPA 2000 and RPR 2001 Interpretation, Guidance and Good Practice* (Lead Editor, John Owen) published by SOLACE/AEA, January 2001.

CHAPTER 3
DIFFERENT KINDS OF ELECTIONS

      A. European Elections
      B. Parliamentary Elections
      C. Welsh Assembly Elections
      D. Greater London Authority Elections
      E. London Borough Elections
      F. County Elections
      G. District, Borough or City Elections
      H. Parish or Town Council Elections
      I. Community Council Elections
      J. Parish and Community Polls
      K. Elected Mayor Referendums
      L. Elected Mayor Elections

In England and Wales there are several different kinds of elections: indeed several different kinds of polls.

Elections and polls are not the same thing. An election is a process for choosing a person to hold a particular office or job; a poll (as the word itself originally implied) is a procedure of counting heads or votes to ascertain winners and losers or decide questions – and sometimes to decide about lost deposits.

If an election is called and only one candidate is validly nominated, or there is only one candidate left at the close of the candidature withdrawal time, that person will be declared elected unopposed without a poll. There is no need for a headcount of who supports whom.

Similarly a referendum is about deciding the answer to a question, not choosing someone to hold office. There is no equivalent of being elected (or "returned") unopposed, and a poll is always necessary to obtain the totals of answers of those entitled to express their preferences by voting or polling.

We will refer to each of the various kinds of elections in turn. On combined elections see chapter 24.

A. EUROPEAN ELECTIONS

Every five years (the last being 10 June 1999) elections are held for the UK's places in the European Parliament. The European Parliamentary Elections Act 1999 abolished the previous 81 European constituencies, which had been formed by grouping the existing parliamentary constituencies into clusters for the purpose. Instead nine regional systems were created, with elections to return a total of 87 MEPs on a proportional list system (counted by the Belgian d'Hondt method), instead of first-past-the post for each European constituency. This was a major change in electoral practice in this country and its significance could be lost in the fact that there was a very low turnout (24%). In 2003, the pre-election year for the European elections due in 2004, the Secretary of State has a duty to see if changes to the list of regions and allocations of MEPs are needed: see para 4 of sch 1 to the 1999 Act.

Each MEP today has therefore not been elected directly: they have been declared elected because first, their political party won enough votes to get one or more seats, and secondly, because they were high enough up their party's list of candidates to take the seat in question. So, in a region electing, say, six MEPs, Party X, entitled to three of those seats when the results are counted and declared, will see the first three of its "slate" of six candidates declared elected.

If an MEP loses or resigns their party whip or membership, they do not thereby lose their seat. But if an MEP dies or loses their seat for a statutory reason (disqualification), then the returning officer is required to declare the next willing candidate on that party's original list elected instead: see para 17 of the European Parliamentary Elections Regulations 1999, S I No 1214.

These are the principal regulations for European elections. They operate in a cumbersome and unreadable way by largely amending the existing Parliamentary law, principally in RPAs 1983 and 1985. SOLACE Enterprises Ltd published a commentary, *The European Parliamentary Elections: The Legislative Framework*, edited by John Turner in 1999 to help set out the new procedural requirements.

The regional returning officers for the European regions were prescribed by the European Parliamentary Elections (Returning Officers) Order 1999, SI No 948. For each Parliamentary constituency within the region the relevant acting returning officer for that constituency is called the local returning officer. For their respective roles, see para 2 of sch 2 to the 1999 Act (substituting para 4 of sch 1 to the European Parliamentary Elections Act 1978) and para 4 of the 1999 Regulations SI No 1214 mentioned above. Thus it was possible for some regional returning officers to be also local returning officers - see section A of chapter 4.

B. PARLIAMENTARY ELECTIONS

The House of Commons is elected for maximum of five years, but MPs are alone in not being elected for a fixed term, because the Prime Minister of the day can ask the Queen to dissolve Parliament and to trigger a general election. Parliament must be sitting when the Prime Minister asks the Queen for a dissolution, making Parliamentary recess dates important. Seventeen working days must elapse between the dissolution of Parliament and polling day as stipulated by RPA 1983. For an example of a Parliamentary election timetable see Appendix 2.

Parliamentary elections are conducted generally under the RPAs 1983 and 1985. Sch 1 to the RPA 1983 is known as the Parliamentary Elections Rules.

The House of Commons currently comprises 659 constituencies, fixed every few years by the Parliamentary Boundary Commission (to become part of the Electoral Commission probably in 2004-05) via a statutory procedure. For historical reasons, the constituencies are divided into county constituencies and borough constituencies, currently set out, as amended by SI 1998 No 3152, in the Parliamentary Constituencies (Wales) and (England) Orders 1995, respectively SIs Nos 1036 and 1626. This makes no practical difference of much consequence (though sub-agents can be appointed in county constituencies – see chapter 11), but the returning officer is different. For county constituencies, the returning officer is the high sheriff of that county; for borough constituencies, it is the appropriate district council chairman or the mayor of the borough (or mayor or lord mayor of a city, as appropriate). Constituency boundaries may well mean that borough or county areas are not exactly coterminous with local government units. Remember that a borough or city with an elected mayor (see K and L below) will as a result have a chairman and not a mayor as its civic figurehead, and it is that chairman, not the elected mayor, who will be the returning officer.

The officer who runs the actual Parliamentary election process is the acting returning officer, on which see s 28 of the 1983 Act.

A Parliamentary election begins with the receipt of a writ from the Clerk of the Crown ordering that an election be held. That writ is returned – hence "returning officer" - when the election is completed and the result declared. The candidate declared elected cannot become an MP unless the Clerk of the Crown has received back the properly completed writ. See also chapter 18 on this procedure.

C. WELSH ASSEMBLY ELECTIONS
Elections to the Welsh Assembly, which comprises ninety seats, are held every four years and next due in May 2003, though the date can be varied by up to a month. They are run under the Government of Wales Act 1998 (see ss 3 and 4).

There are five Assembly electoral regions, corresponding with the five Welsh European constituencies as they were before the European Parliamentary Elections Act 1999 (see sch 1 to the 1998 Act). Each region returns four Assembly seats; there is also one member for each of the forty Assembly constituencies (which correspond with the Parliamentary constituencies). See the National Assembly for Wales (Representation of the People) Order 1999, SI No 450.

Each Welsh voter has two votes: one vote for an Assembly constituency candidate under the simple majority system ("first past the post"), and one for a regional registered political party list with the election held under the additional member system of proportional representation.

D. GREATER LONDON AUTHORITY ELECTIONS
Following a London referendum, the Greater London Authority was established by the Greater London Authority Act 1999.

The Authority consists of the Mayor of London, directly elected for the first time in May 2000, and twenty-five members together comprising the London Assembly. Of these twenty-five, fourteen are members for Assembly constituencies and eleven are members at large for the whole of Greater London. They are known respectively as "constituency members" and "London members": see s 2 of the 1999 Act. The term of office of the Mayor and all assembly members is four years, so that the next elections are due in May 2004.

The Mayor is returned under the simple majority system ("first past the post") unless there are more than three candidates, when a supplementary vote system of first and second preferences applies. But each elector has three votes: one for the Mayor; one for their Assembly constituency on a simple majority "first past the post" basis; and one for a list of registered political party candidates (or for an individual candidate) for Greater London as a whole. The rules for counting those votes are set out in Part II of sch 2 to the 1999 Act, sch 3 to which amends the RPA 1983 in relation to these kinds of election. No one may be a candidate in more than one Assembly constituency: s 4 (9). Nor can someone already elected as Mayor or as a constituency member be also elected as a London member of the Assembly: see para 8(4) of Part II of sch 2 to the 1999 Act.

The Assembly constituencies are prescribed under s 2 (4) of the 1999 Act by the Greater London Authority (Assembly Constituencies and Returning Officers) Order 1999, SI No 3380.

E. LONDON BOROUGH COUNCIL ELECTIONS
London Borough Council elections for the 32 London Boroughs established by the London Government Act 1963 are run under rules essentially similar to those for county and district councils elsewhere, on which see sections F and G following.

The City of London has some special provisions of its own but is largely brought into the scope of the same provisions as other municipal elections by s 191 of the RPA 1983.

F. COUNTY ELECTIONS
County Council elections, i.e. elections to county councils comprising a tier of two-tier local government, are held every four years and are next due on 3 May 2001 (and after that in May 2005). They are run under the RPA 1983 and the Local Elections Rules, i.e. principally the Local Elections (Principal Areas) Rules 1986, SI No 2214, as last amended by SI 2000 No 81.

Counties are divided into electoral divisions, prescribed for each county by a statutory instrument made following a review by the Local Government Commission (to become part of the Electoral Commission in April 2002). (There are now no counties outside England.) These electoral divisions are the equivalent of wards for district or borough (city) elections, and may indeed have the same names or areas in some cases, but unlike many wards, electoral divisions currently elect only one councillor each. Section 89 of the Local Government Act 2000 amends ss 14 and 17 of the Local Government Act 1992 to enable county electoral divisions to have more than one councillor in future (and see also G below on ss 84-7 of the 2000 Act). The Government in its white paper *Local Leadership, Local Choice* suggested that a way of enhancing local democracy was to increase the number of elections - indeed, to allow the electorate to vote annually in some form of local election, hence the aforementioned powers.

The returning officer for the county is that authority's proper officer (see chapter 4). In practice the returning officer is likely to delegate much of the task of actually manning the procedures to counterparts in the constituent county districts.

G. DISTRICT, BOROUGH OR CITY ELECTIONS
This heading refers to district councils in the English two-tier system. Possession of borough or city status makes no practical difference for this purpose.

District council elections are held, according to the choice made by the council or prescribed by order, either every four years (the next due in May 2003) for the whole council, or every year other than the county election year for a third of the council. Sections 84-86 of the Local Government Act 2000 allow the existing patterns of whole council elections or elections by thirds to be varied, and for the Secretary of State to alter by order under s 87 the years in which elections are held. District elections are run under the same legislation and rules as county elections, on which see section F above.

Districts are divided into wards, likewise prescribed for each district by a statutory instrument following a review by the Local Government Commission (to become part of the Electoral Commission in April 2002).

The returning officer for district elections is that authority's proper officer (see chapter 4).

H. PARISH OR TOWN COUNCIL ELECTIONS

Parish councils have whole-council elections every four years, usually on the same day as district councils (see s 16 (as amended) of the Local Government Act 1972). Town councils are effectively parish councils with town council status, which does not affect their election arrangements at all. Parish council elections are on occasion delayed if a general election is to be held on what would otherwise be a parish (and district) election day – as on 3 May 1979, when the delay was effected by s 2 (1) of the RPA 1979.

Larger parishes are sometimes divided into wards, which will either have been prescribed by the statutory instrument establishing the parish arrangement or by the district council in whose area the parish is situated. (Parishes have to be wholly contained within one district council area, and can be comprised within metropolitan borough or unitary authority areas as well, but not London Boroughs.)

The returning officer for parish elections is the proper officer appointed for the purpose of the district council within which the parish is contained. Where parishes do not have councils, but only parish meetings (in which all the local government electors can meet together: see section J of this chapter), they do not have elections.

Parish councils are the only councils which can co-opt members. This can occur if either insufficient candidates stand at the main elections, or when a vacancy occurs. The first case is prescribed by s 21 of the RPA 1985; secondly, in the case of a casual vacancy, the parish clerk must publish a notice giving the parish electors fourteen days (i.e. days valid for election timetable purposes – see rule 2 of Part I of sch 2 to the Local Elections (Parish and Committees) Rules 1986, SI No 2215, as last amended by SI 2001 No 80) during which to requisition an election. If ten electors sign a requisition, a by-election will be held; if not, the parish council can co-opt a local elector, i.e. someone who would have been entitled to stand as a candidate in an actual election, to become a parish councillor. See para 8 of the 1986 Rules, which prescribe the running of parish and community elections which are uncombined with any other elections.

I. COMMUNITY COUNCIL ELECTIONS

Community councils are the Welsh equivalent of English parish councils. The election rules and circumstances are essentially the same for both, save in respect of Welsh language usage. See s 35 of the Local Government Act 1972 (as amended).

J. PARISH AND COMMUNITY POLLS

Parish polls are a kind of referendum, though their results are not binding in the strict legal sense. They are held under para 18(2) of Part III of sch 12 to the Local Government Act 1972 and only apply to parish meetings, and the Welsh equivalent community meetings (see para 34(2) of Part II of sch 12 to the 1972 Act).

A poll can be held where under para 18(4) or a third (whichever is the less) of the local government electors present so demand.

A notice must be given to the district council proper officer to conduct a poll on the submitted question under the Parish and Community Meetings (Polls) Rules 1987, SI No 1, as amended by SI 1987 No 262. The parish or community meeting requiring the poll has to pay for it; the district council will fix a scale of charges, including returning officer fees.

There has been a recent trend for certain parishes to require polls on national or general topics that are not specific to that parish in the immediate sense. Robust opinion has it that the parish poll procedure was not intended for this purpose, but mainly as a way of validating or authorising the collective view of electors of a parish. S 9 (1) of the Local Government Act 1972 specifically states that ". . . there shall be a parish meeting for the purpose of discussing parish affairs . . ." The argument then proceeds on the basis that, for example, the national currency of the United Kingdom is not an affair of the parish, it is an affair of the nation.

It has to be said, however, that this view is not undisputed. Indeed, the National Association of Local Councils do not support it and there are difficult issues around, for instance, GM crops being grown in certain fields within the parish - surely usage of that field is a local, not national matter? In the equivalent provisions of the former Local Government Act 1933 (paras 4 and 5 of Part VI of sch 3) the parish poll provision was based on the power that "A parish meeting may discuss parish affairs and pass resolutions thereon", but such wording does not appear in the 1972 Act. The issue was discussed in relation to the 1933 Act in *Bennett v Chappell* [1966] Ch 391; [1965] 3 All E.R. 130, C.A.

These problems were also considered in 2000 when some parish polls were apparently conducted on national issues (eg UK currency) but other districts refused. The issue did not proceed into the courts and remains unresolved.

Some examples of parish polls held on wider topics are quoted in *Parish Government 1894-1994* by KP Poole and Bryan Keith-Lucas (National Association of Local Councils, 1994), pp 247-8. On the Parish and Community Meetings (Polls) Rules 1987 see Home Office Circular RPA 308 issued on 17 February 1987.

K. ELECTED MAYOR REFERENDUMS

The Local Government Act 2000 introduced the possibility of referendums on whether councils should in principle have elected mayors. This applies in both England and Wales: the principal provisions are ss 34-36 and 45 of the 2000 Act.

A referendum is a necessary step before a council can adopt the elected mayor approach for its executive arrangements. The Secretary of State can direct that a referendum be held (s 35), or require it by order (s 36). A referendum must also be held if an authority receives a valid petition or combination of petitions (s 34), but none of these provisions apply to an authority whose population at the end of June 1999 was under 85,000.

Petitions in England are governed by the Local Authorities (Referendums) (Petitions and Directions) (England) Regulations 2000, SI No 2852. The proper officer must publish at the outset and each year thereafter the verification number. That number, five per cent of the local government electorate (including monthly claims under the Regulations in force up to 2001) is the number of signatures required for a valid petition. Separately the fact of publishing the notices must be published in at least one local newspaper – see paras 4 and 5 of the 2000 Regulations, which are very detailed. Paras 11 and 13 in particular deal with the procedure for the proper officer on receiving a petition, and publicity for that receipt.

The rules for running referendums are set out in the draft Local Authorities (Conduct of Referendums) (England) Regulations 2001, where the responsible manager of the poll process is called the "counting officer", not the returning officer, although in fact para 11 designates as counting officer the RPA 1983, s 35 (3) returning officer for local elections (see chapter 4). As to combined elections, see paras 14-17 (and chapter 24). Basically if the referendum timetable would yield a poll date within 28 days either side of a European, Parliamentary or ordinary local election, the polls must be combined (para 14 (11)).

For Wales equivalent regulations will apply, but are not yet drafted.

L. ELECTED MAYOR ELECTIONS

Once it has been determined following a successful referendum under K above that an elected mayor is to be elected, that election will be conducted (for a four-year term) under ss 39-44 of the Local Government Act 2000. With necessary adaptations, the election is conducted like other local elections under E F and G above.

CHAPTER 4
RETURNING OFFICERS AND DEPUTIES

This chapter follows chapter 3 in providing a short summarising key to who is which returning officer for the different kinds of elections described in that chapter. The different capacity in which you may act for different elections is often confusing to those new to election management.

The same list of twelve different kinds of elections or polls in England and Wales therefore applies:

    A. European Elections
    B. Parliamentary Elections
    C. Welsh Assembly Elections
    D. Greater London Authority Elections
    E. London Borough Elections
    F. County Elections
    G. District, Borough or City Elections
    H. Parish or Town Council Elections
    I. Community Council Elections
    J. Parish and Community Polls
    K. Elected Mayor Referendums
    L. Elected Mayor Elections

A. EUROPEAN ELECTIONS

For each European election region (see map at appendix 4), the Secretary of State prescribes a Parliamentary constituency whose acting returning officer is the regional returning officer. See the European Parliamentary Elections (Returning Officer) Order 1999 SI No 948, derived from the amended sch 1 to the European Parliamentary Elections Act 1978.

Within each Parliamentary constituency comprising part of an European election region, the acting returning officer for that constituency is the local returning officer: see reg 2 of the European Parliamentary Elections Regulations 1999, SI No 1214.

Therefore, in some constituencies one person will be both regional and local returning officer. However, in 1999, in some regions local returning officers were specially appointed for this election by their authorities as a one-off to enable the usual acting returning officer to concentrate upon regional duties. Practice varied across the country.

B. PARLIAMENTARY ELECTIONS

The returning officer for county constituencies (see chapter 3) is the high sheriff of that county, and for borough constituencies is the relevant district chairman or the (lord) mayor of that borough or city – see s 24 of the RPA 1983. But this is a ceremonial role, confined to receiving and returning the writ and declaring the result: see s 27. It is important to remember that returning officers so designated have no authority over the electoral process.

The substantive duties are carried out by an acting returning officer, who is the appropriate (electoral) registration officer – see s 28. Under s 28 (3) the returning officer must give the acting returning officer a notice of duties under rule 50 of the Parliamentary Elections Rules (sch 1 to the RPA 1983) not later than the day after the writ is received. Rule 50 is simply about declaring the result and returning the writ.

Registration officers are appointed under s 8 of the RPA 1983 by London Boroughs, districts or boroughs/cities and unitary and metropolitan councils in England (plus the City of London), and counties and county boroughs in Wales.

C. WELSH ASSEMBLY ELECTIONS

Para 16(1) of the National Assembly for Wales (Representation of the People) Order 1999, SI No 450 prescribes a constituency returning officer for each Assembly constituency, who is either the relevant county or county borough returning officer or in a cross-boundary case the one designated by the Assembly.

Para 16(1) also prescribes a regional returning officer for each Assembly electoral region, who is the appropriate county or county borough returning officer designated by the Assembly. See paras 17-21 for ancillary returning officer provisions.

D. GREATER LONDON AUTHORITY ELECTIONS

The returning officer for elections for the Mayor of London and London members of the London Assembly is the proper officer of the Greater London Authority: see s 35 (2C) of the RPA 1983, inserted by para 3(2) of sch 3 to the Greater London Authority Act 1999. However, special arrangements were put in place for the election of the first mayor (Ken Livingstone) in 2000 as the GLA officers were not yet appointed.

For constituency members (see chapter 3) the returning officer is designated by the Secretary of State, being from the appropriate London borough: see s 35(2B) of the 1983 Act as similarly inserted, and the Greater London Authority (Assembly Constituencies and Returning Officers) Order 1999, SI No 3380.

E. LONDON BOROUGH ELECTIONS
For London borough elections, the returning officer is appointed by the council under s 35 (3) of the RPA 1983 as the proper officer for that purpose. The "proper officer" is a person defined by s 270 (3) and (4) of the Local Government Act 1972.

F. COUNTY ELECTIONS
For county councils, the returning officer is appointed by the council under s 35 (1) of the RPA 1983. That person will usually appoint deputies to run each constituent district group election for the relevant county electoral divisions. Such deputies will ordinarily be the equivalent returning officer in those constituent authorities.

Generally, it is the chief executive or county secretary and solicitor (or holder of the equivalently named post) who is the county returning officer. It is custom and practice to appoint district returning officers to undertake the election in their particular areas. However, it must be fairly said, this is not universally followed throughout the country. It is not unknown for service level agreements or memoranda of understanding to exist between the county returning officer and the district deputy defining the particular roles and responsibilities, mainly at district level.

G. DISTRICT, BOROUGH OR CITY ELECTIONS
As for county councils, the returning officer is appointed by the council under s 35 (1) of the RPA 1983. The civic status has no significant impact on election procedures.

H. PARISH OR TOWN COUNCIL ELECTIONS
The returning officer for parish or town council elections is appointed under s 35 (1) of the RPA 1983 by the district, borough or city council for the area within which the parish or town council is situated. The

wording implies that the same person shall be appointed for all parish or town councils within such an area.

I. COMMUNITY COUNCILS
The returning officer for community council elections in Wales is appointed by the county or county borough council within which the community is situated: see s 35 (1A) of the RPA 1983. As for H above the wording implies that the same person shall be appointed for all community councils within such an area.

J. PARISH AND COMMUNITY POLLS
A returning officer is appointed under rule 4(1) of the Parish and Community Meetings (Polls) Rules 1987, SI No 1 by the district, borough or city (England) or county or county borough (Wales) council within whose area the parish or community in question is situated. The district or borough council must in turn "appoint an officer for the purpose of the poll" (rule 4(3)).

The wording implies that a separate appointment should technically be made for each time a poll is lawfully demanded, but, usually, when someone is appointed chief executive they receive a generic appointment to become returning officer for elections and parish polls generally. It is worth checking the contract of appointment but is not common to have separate and new appointments.

K. ELECTED MAYOR REFERENDUMS
The person managing a referendum for an elected mayor is styled the counting officer (under the Referendum Act 1975 the person in overall charge for each area was called the chief counting officer). The person who is the counting officer is the person who is ordinarily the RPA 1983 s 35 (3) returning officer for local elections: see E above and para 11 (1) of the draft Local Authorities (Conduct of Referendums) (England) Regulations 2001.

For Wales equivalent regulations will apply.

L. ELECTED MAYOR ELECTIONS
The returning officer for the election of an elected mayor is the person who is the returning officer under E F or G above for that council's ordinary local government elections.

A returning officer (or acting returning officer) should always appoint at least one deputy. This is a personal, not council, appointment, and should be specific to each election (you never know when you may be ill, incapacitated, or just out of the office).

Deputies are appointed under the appropriate statutory authorities – e.g. s 28 (5) of the RPA 1983 for Parliamentary elections, and s 35 (4) of the 1983 Act for local elections. It is good practice to appoint a deputy for all purposes; it may also be useful to appoint one or more additional deputies for limited purposes such as receiving and adjudicating on nomination papers, or conducting the count (necessary if more than one venue is to be used). Returning officers often talk about giving their deputies full or limited powers delegations. Shaw and Sons Ltd and some software systems will provide forms for this purpose. (Technically a deputy cannot appoint further deputies, so a district chief executive in a county election should ask the county returning officer to do this.)

Your status as returning officer or deputy etc. is important for other reasons. Service as a deputy returning officer is not pensionable, but service as a returning (or acting) returning officer is pensionable, as is also a regional and/or local returning officer role in European elections. Why the difference?

That difference is contained in reg 4 of the Local Government Pension Scheme Regulations 1997, SI No 1612. To be eligible to pay pension contributions and receive benefits, you have to be employed by a "Scheme employer", i.e. basically a body (including ordinary local authorities) listed in sch 2 to the 1997 Regulations. As a deputy returning officer is a personal appointment made not by the council but by an individual returning officer who is not a Scheme employer as defined, such service is not reckonable service as an "active member" of a pension scheme.

If returning officer service is pensionable, always pay the contributions, and check that your employing council pays the relevant employer contribution (recovering their costs wherever possible from the Home Office for Parliamentary or European elections and similarly for the Welsh Assembly). On retirement, pension entitlement from election work is separate from a main local government job: the calculations have differing rules and any added years are similarly added separately. (It is possible in principle for different numbers of added years to be added for the distinct employments.) On these rules see the Association of Local Authority Chief Executives *ALACE Guidance Notes* (undated, but published in 2000), especially pp 7-9. The fashion nowadays is to consolidate election payments within the overall salary package, prior to retirement, as this enhances available years, thus increasing the value of the pension. This practice has been accepted by superannuation authorities (not without difficulties in some areas) but it is important to consider it well in advance of retirement.

The most frequently occurring situation is for an English district chief executive to be a local returning officer for the European elections, acting for a Parliamentary, deputy for a county, and returning officer for district and parish elections. This apparent confusion will soon become second nature!

CHAPTER 5
POLLING DISTRICTS AND POLLING PLACES

Under s 18 of the RPA 1983 parliamentary constituencies must be divided into polling districts and polling places. This section sets out requirements as to how arrangements must be made so that voters have, so far as practicable, similarly convenient facilities or distances for going to vote according to the topography and local circumstances. The polling districts also serve for compiling the electoral register and for running all kinds of elections.

Districts have to be wholly contained within district wards or county electoral divisions, so that if their boundaries are not contiguous the pattern of polling districts will have to be compatible with both sets of boundaries. It is the council which determines the districts, by order, and "an alteration of polling districts shall not be effective until the coming into force of the first register prepared from electors lists published after the alteration is made", i.e. prepared from the draft register: see s 18 (8) of the 1983 Act, relating to the pre-RPR 2001 electoral register procedure.

The council similarly fixes polling places by order under the RPA 1983 s 18, but in this case they can be altered at any time. Whereas the polling district is a convenient sub-division of the parliamentary constituency, the polling place is a designated location or area within which the actual polling, at the polling station, must take place. Where polling district or polling place changes are made, that must be advertised publicly: see s 18 (6) of the 1983 Act.

A polling place may be either quite tightly defined or a wider area: indeed frequently a polling place may be designated as the whole of a polling district. On that depends where the actual polling station itself is located: a polling station will usually be a single room or building: if the polling place is a single building or location, that means that the polling station must be there too. If the polling place is a wider area, or the whole of the polling district, it leaves more scope for placing (or moving) the actual polling station within the scope of the polling place definition.

Whereas the council fixes the polling districts and places, under rule 20(1) of the Local Elections (Principal Area) Rules 1986, SI No 2214 it is for the returning officer (or, in the case of Parliamentary elections, the acting returning officer) to fix the location of polling stations (see chapter 6). That is simply an administrative act, requiring no particular powers or timetable in itself: nevertheless it is certainly good practice to invite comments before acting.

The council should consider advertising any proposals to make a new order for polling districts or polling places, and consulting whichever political parties are active locally. That will reduce the likelihood of arguments or difficulties later once the final decisions have been made. Reference has already been made to the duty to publish a notice of changes made under s 18 (6).

It is likely that returning officers will want to arrange more polling stations, where they have the flexibility to do so, for elections where a high turnout is expected. Often this will amount to doubling up two stations in the same premises, which is quite permissible and needs no prior notice or formality.

It is important for newly appointed proper officers/returning officers to check for themselves the status, circumstances and mapping, of their polling districts, places and stations. To leave this until an election is called is to risk problems that cannot then be corrected. A "non-compliance" with s 18, or "any informality relative to polling districts or polling places" will not call an election into question (s 18 (9)), but this is a procedural safeguard only: a fundamental failure to make proper provision for what is required is a very serious matter and would be likely to render the whole proceeding void.

CHAPTER 6

POLLING STATIONS

The previous chapter has dealt with polling districts and polling places; this is concerned with polling stations. To repeat the definitions:

(i) a polling district is a geographical part of a Parliamentary constituency defined by an order sub-dividing that constituency for the convenience and essentially similar treatment of voters;

(ii) a polling place is an area or location for, but not necessarily within, a polling district defined by an order within which polling station(s) must be contained; and

(iii) a polling station is the actual room or similar space within which actual voting or polling takes place.

Rule 20(1) of the Local Elections (Principal Areas) Regulations 1986 SI No 2214, provides that "The returning officer shall provide a sufficient number of polling stations and ... shall allot the electors to the polling stations in such manner as he thinks most convenient".

Local practice will inevitably vary as to the choice and arrangement of polling stations. Beyond the general principles that govern the creation of polling places, there are few rules about their logistics (as opposed to opening hours, what notices to display, etc.). The number of stations must be adequate: one station might be quite adequate, for, say, 1250 electors if you expect a 30% turnout over thirteen hours at a local election, but need doubling up for a likely 75% turnout over fifteen hours at a Parliamentary election. Similarly, the first station might have a presiding officer (compulsory) and one polling clerk: but two poll clerks might be necessary in the second case to allow the staff both to keep proper control without too much queuing and also to take proper breaks during a long day. The returning officer can preside at a station in person (see rule 21 of the 1986 Regulations), but this would be very exceptional: such responsibilities may restrict the possibility of necessary response to whatever else arises.

Polling stations need to be reasonably suitable for their purpose, and have access for the disabled. That also includes people who are so-called "semi-ambulant" – an elderly person, for instance, may find a long walk in from the pavement just as much of a deterrent as steps are to a wheelchair user or a parent with a pushchair. The polling station staff need mobile or other telephones to summon help urgently if needed – if possible a non-public line to the election office so that they can more readily get through in case of need. There should be clear demarcation if the polling stations are in the same room, with the ballot boxes positioned to lessen the chance of crossover voting. Each station needs three or four booths at least – ideally one of which should be lower to facilitate use by someone in a wheelchair.

It is good practice to invite regularly participating local parties to express any views about the location of polling stations. In any event, the more active local party workers (very often elected members of your authority) put forward their own views without specific invitation. Those views should not determine, but can sometimes reasonably influence, the outcome. Similarly polling stations need to be checked for anything that might give rise to any perception of prejudice – voters must have a calm and unpressured place in which to vote.

Usually the polling station will only be the actual room or hall etc. where the actual voting takes place. There may well be a connecting corridor to a hallway, or to the open air, and these will be outside what is legally the polling station itself. The presiding officer should nevertheless take care to ensure that such accesses are kept properly marked, clear of obstructions and not unduly invaded by noise or unofficial party scrutineers (see chapter 17) – even if it is raining!

Under rule 22 of the Parliamentary Elections Rules (RPA 1983, sch 1) returning officers have the right to requisition certain schools and public rooms funded from the public purse to use as polling stations. The public rooms are those "the expense of maintaining which is payable out of any rate". The simplicity of the schools definition has blurred in recent years as some colleges (and the former grant-maintained schools) have left the traditional education authority control. Nevertheless it will still include large numbers of LEA schools. It covers "a school maintained or assisted by a local education authority . . . or a school in respect of which grants are made out of monies provided by Parliament to the person or body of persons responsible for the management of the school." There are similar provisions applicable for other sorts of elections.

Use of these, especially in May as summer examinations loom, is increasingly and understandably resisted by schools, but often their use is hard to avoid because of their situation at the heart of local housing estates and communities. Often returning officers are under pressure to use a particular mobile classroom, for instance, and allow the rest of the school to operate as normal. This is becoming increasingly commonplace but can lead to problems at, for example, 4pm when school buses and cars bringing electors compete for the same parking spaces, occasionally with some disregard for the safety of pupils and others.

Where schools are used, both the school itself and the presiding officer may experience security problems. Check that all the usual routes are open: if a school back gate is padlocked at the start of polling, all the locals who expect to use that access may be effectively denied entry, or have to go a very long way round. That will inevitably lead to problems and accusations.

Finding suitable polling station premises in rural areas regularly causes returning officers problems. Some villages (even larger settlements) have little choice and can only offer some venerable facility with poor access for the disabled, no car parking and even only intermittent electricity and water. The poll must go ahead and so such alternatives as caravans and portakabins should be considered, although on grounds of health, safety and general convenience the least worst choice is often highly unsatisfactory. Recriminations are vividly reported in the local media (let alone complaints from staff) who are not always sympathetic to the returning officer's problems, but such is the nature of this work.

Note that the law prescribes who may lawfully be in a polling station. It is legally the presiding officer, not the returning officer, in whose control the station is. This should be borne in mind when visiting the station or dealing with public order and other similar issues. It is also a relevant consideration for insurance purposes. (It is the presiding officer's duty to keep order at a polling station – see rule 33 of the Parliamentary Elections Rules – sch 1 to the RPR 1983 – and elsewhere such as SI 1986 No 2214 para 27; 1986 No 2215 para 27; and 1999 No 450 Rule 38 of sch 5.)

CHAPTER 7
THINGS TO DO FIRST FOR ELECTIONS; AND CASUAL VACANCIES

This chapter operates as a short checklist of things to do at the outset of, or immediately before, an election process. The activities themselves are discussed in the other chapters.

In practice the activities will often proceed simultaneously rather than sequentially: time is short, so responses have to be prompt. That time element predicates the first requirement: to check the election timetable, which will effectively map out the process of the ensuing few weeks. (See the timetables in appendices 2 and 3.)

Obviously it is easiest to prepare for fixed date elections such as the European Parliamentary or local polls. At its shortest a Parliamentary election can be called in just over three weeks, whereas the timetable for ordinary local government elections is nearly twice as long at over five weeks counting down to the first Thursday in May. For main elections a timetable will probably be supplied from elsewhere, and be almost the same for everyone, but of course for local by-elections you have to work it out for yourself. We say "almost the same" because there is some limited room for local discretion over sending and opening absent votes etc., but all the key dates – close of nominations, polling etc. – will be the same.

Only weekdays are valid days to count in the election timetable, and in addition certain Bank Holidays and others like Maundy Thursday, have also to be left out of account (described as *dies non*). Clearly almost all elections running up to the first Thursday in May will see a number of such days discounted. As to election days and timetable, see rule 2 of the Parliamentary Elections Rules (i.e. sch 1 to the RPA 1983), and similarly elsewhere (e.g. rule 2 of SIs 1986 Nos 2214 and 2215 for local, parish and community elections).

The second initial step must be to check or arrange adequate insurances, as advised in chapter 8. Once these preliminaries are in place, other immediate requirements include:

(i) publishing the notice of election;
(ii) appointing one or more deputies to assist or take over from you;
(iii) arranging to appoint election staff;
(iv) liasing with the election agents known at that stage;
(v) booking rooms etc. to be used as polling stations;
(vi) booking somewhere suitable to hold the count;
(vii) checking that all the required polling equipment and stationery is available and ordered;
(viii) checking where you can get quotes for printing ballot papers, a highly responsible task in itself. (Printing ballot papers takes time, as they are produced in "cheque book" format and reasonably specialist equipment is needed for the sequential numbering together with perforations. It is the authors' experience that this is rarely undertaken by in-house print units, though they often tackle other tasks such as notices of poll, nominations, etc.);
(ix) assessing the public relations/press and media requirements;
(x) arranging to supply free copies of electoral registers as required – see the RPR 2001, SI No 341 para 47.

Although there will be much else to do (and some things, like booking a room for the count, may have been done months earlier), sorting out the items on the list will get a grip on the election process from the outset, and help to ensure that in the busy and often stressful time ahead no vital step is forgotten or runs late with potentially disastrous consequences.

By-elections for European, Parliamentary or Welsh Assembly elections are triggered at the relevant national level. For local government elections, see ss 84 – 89 of the Local Government Act 1972, noting where, through its proper officer, the authority has to declare a vacancy. Ordinarily a notice from two electors for the area is needed to trigger an election: see s 89 (1) (6). "Area" here means "principal area" as defined in s 270 (1) of the 1972 Act, i.e. that whole council area not just the relevant ward or county electoral division where the casual vacancy occurred. See also the second part of Home Office Circular RPA 321 (published on 2 February 1988) on a notice from two electors received before a notice of casual vacancy has been published (considered to be a valid requirement for an election to be held).

Note that if a local, parish or community election vacancy occurs within six months of the end of the fixed term of office, no by-election will be held: see e.g. s 89 (3) of the Local Government Act 1972. This is a common type of provision for fixed term elections.

On filling Welsh Assembly casual vacancies, see s 8 of the Government of Wales Act 1998 for Assembly constituency seats, and s 9 of that Act for Assembly electoral region seats.

On filling casual vacancies in the office of Mayor of London see s 16 of the Greater London Authority Act 1999; and on casual vacancies of seats in the Assembly constituencies generally or of London Assembly members, see ss 10 and 11 of the 1999 Act.

CHAPTER 8

INSURANCE

It is a cardinal rule of running elections that you must have proper and adequate insurance. This should always be checked before the start of any election process. The rubric is do not even dream of running elections without proper insurance. High Court litigation costs are very substantial.

In this increasingly litigious age, protecting yourself against the possibility of expensive legal action does not need underlining. What may bear repetition, however, is the personal and separate nature of the role of the returning officer. That means that any action taken to question the validity of the returning officer's decision, or the proper conduct of the election process, will be taken against the returning officer personally. Fully adequate insurance is accordingly essential.

For the 1999 European elections SOLACE obtained a block policy from which regional and local returning officers could benefit. The Home Office will not allow the returning officer the cost of personal elections insurance (an anachronistic outlook in modern circumstances it may be thought). Authorities can, however, quite properly arrange to pay for such insurance for whoever they appoint their proper officer for European and Parliamentary elections, and should do so for all other elections; reasonably commonplace is an extension of the council's general officials indemnity policy. However it is done, returning officers should check policy terms for themselves.

As a guide, the level of liability cover should be no less than £1m being the limit quoted for one of the authors' officials indemnity policy. The cover for the European election policy referred to above was fixed at up to £2m. (As a national policy it was, technically, susceptible to a greater extent of claim.)

So far we have referred to the returning officer's personal liability in the context of challenged decisions or judicial review, election petitions and so on. Another important aspect, however, is the returning officer's liability in respect of all the other employees and situations which may arise. Imagine that an employee working at a polling station is assaulted by a voter or otherwise injured while on duty; or that a voter trips over rough paving at the door of the polling station premises; or that at the count someone claims they have wrongly been excluded by the security staff when they had a right or a ticket to be admitted. In each case the returning officer may have a claim to defend, and will require insurance accordingly. Even if these occurrences happen to council employees or on council premises they are unlikely to come within the scope of ordinary council corporate insurances because of the distinct separate nature of the election process as an activity. Remember that elections staff are employed in your name as returning officer, not in the name of the council (see chapter 9). Sometimes there are some tricky problems over car insurance as to whether or not individual policies cover elections staff whilst driving to the polling station but extensive discussion of such matters is well beyond our scope here. Again, there always seem to be staff who, somehow, manage to damage either their person or their clothing on, for example, elderly village hall furniture. These matters result in small claims and, regrettably, arguments over excess limits on various insurance policies. Local situations vary and it is worthwhile being aware of policy applications.

As an approximate guide, the amount of cover required for such purposes should not be less than that quoted above.

CHAPTER 9

APPOINTING ELECTION STAFF

Elections officers will normally keep lists of people who are willing and suitable for elections work – particularly for election day appointments as polling station presiding officers, poll clerks and for running the count afterwards. This is essential: a Parliamentary election, for example, can easily require in excess of three hundred people on the day, and without a starting point it would be extremely difficult to make that many appointments in the statutory time available.

Appointments are personal to the returning officer (or deputy or local returning officer in the case of county or European elections for instance), so again it is worthwhile underlining the point (see chapter 8) about having them and yourself adequately insured. They are made under rule 26 of the Parliamentary Elections Rules (sch 1 to the RPA 1983) and equivalent provisions for other elections.

Local practice and expectation will no doubt play a considerable part in who is appointed. Obviously people should not be excluded from appointment on inappropriate grounds: so long as they have the right experience or aptitude, and can physically do whatever has to be done – perhaps with the assistance of one or more other polling station staff – then there should be no problem.

Many returning officers try to avoid appointing someone as a presiding officer if they have not served as a poll clerk once or twice before, but this will not always be possible, especially for last minute appointments. Since the European elections of 1999 there has been better provision for training polling station staff (and particularly presiding officers), and a greater likelihood of fees or pay being made available to get people together for the training time involved.

Election staff should not be generally associated with a particular political party or viewpoint, though of course formal political restriction under section 2 of the Local Government, Planning and Housing Act 1989 is not required (though that probably would be appropriate for the permanent Election Office employees). Needless to say, on polling day itself they must be scrupulously impartial, and may need to be reminded about coming dressed in particular colours or styles, or behaving in any other way, which could give rise to an allegation of bias.

Commonly local government officers staff elections with recently retired employees and a variety of others known to or connected with the Election Office in some way. Avoid any sense of special relationships or patronage – though often this can be countered by recognition that overall the requisite staff are in short supply. Sometimes the assumption is made that people can readily be found from the unemployed register: indeed they may, but it will not always be easy to find people with the necessary attributes and sense of impartiality. Nor are many people willing to de-register and re-register to legitimise working for just one day for a not particularly high fee, though this latter factor is evidently an issue for them rather than for you the employing returning officer.

It is worthwhile referring here to a couple of issues that regularly trouble returning officers over staff appointments. Should council employees (of whatever grading) be allowed a day off at the grace of the employing authority or should they be required to take holiday? The latter school of thought maintains they should not be paid twice (ie usual salary and election fee) and prays in aid the competitive requirements of many council (tendered) contracts such as leisure and refuse. The former theory is built around the notions that it is difficult to recruit staff for election duties, election fees after tax are not hugely generous and you need to be able to rely on regular core staff knowledgeable in matters electoral. Practice varies locally, but the "free day off" situation generally prevails, albeit with varying degrees of co-operation from colleague chief officers who have targets to meet and understandable service delivery pressures upon them.

Again, it is important to have some monitoring over the age of staff recruited for these duties. This is not to be unfashionably (and politically incorrect) "ageist" but simply cognisant of the fact that insurance policies regularly exclude those over certain ages - 65 and 70 are not uncommon and some policies require specific consent to be obtained. It is prudent to have such matters checked. A number of returning officers encourage younger staff, particularly at the count, and make approaches to local colleges - however, National Insurance numbers will be required and reflection upon safe travel arrangements is sensible.

Many returning officers believe it is better to avoid using the same people to count at night as have been out in polling stations during the day, particularly for the longer polling hours of 7am to 10pm. Even if they are not infringing the Working Time Directive, they will be tired, unable to get to the count immediately because of their polling station closedown responsibilities, and particularly at risk of diminishing concentration if the count or recount is protracted. However, some returning officers take the contrary view - presiding officers have to bring their boxes in anyway and, at some devolved rural counts (some districts may run 8 to 10 scattered counts separately on one night), it is often easier to ask presiding officers to stay on to count. If there are problems over a ballot paper account there are advantages in having the presiding officer present for further enquiries to be made. It is a classic - and typical - example of the returning officer having to decide upon the most workable solution for the local circumstances.

Bank employees and others with manual dexterity are popular appointees for counts for obvious reasons, but such skills are rare in these days of automatic teller machines. Be that as it may, the question of impartiality still applies, even if rather less rigidly for counting assistants than, say, for supervisors or those helping to arrange the overall process.

In many areas it is increasingly difficult to persuade people to agree to work at counts, especially in inner cities, because of the times and personal security issues involved set beside relatively low fees. Nevertheless there is often a considerable pressure from local precedent and candidate expectation influencing the returning officer to count at night directly after polls close wherever possible – but this not a legal requirement.

It is good practice and recommended that returning officers hold a briefing meeting for, at least, all presiding officers prior to election day, usually when they attend at the council offices to collect their ballot boxes. Again, local practice can vary but it is often worthwhile having poll clerks in attendance too. Such meetings are commonly held a day or two before polling day or, more rarely nowadays, very early in the morning on polling day itself. It is a positive sign to election staff that you as returning officer are interested in their work, intend to lead them forward through the process and can at least listen to their queries even if unable to fully answer all their questions.

CHAPTER 10
WORKING WITH ELECTION AGENTS

Candidates generally have to appoint election agents (RPA 1983, s 67), though they will actually be, or be deemed to be, their own agent in some cases: see s 70 (1) of the 1983 Act. In a county (but not borough) Parliamentary constituency one sub-agent may be appointed: ss 68-69. In European elections several sub-agents may be appointed under a national agent: see paras 10-14 of the European Parliamentary Elections Regulations 1999, SI No 1214. See also paras 32-35 of SI 1999 No 450 for the Welsh Assembly, and paras 11-15 of Part 1 of sch 1 to the Greater London authority Act for 1999 for those elections.

It will not always be clear at the outset of an election process or campaign which parties or individuals will be standing. This need not inhibit dealing and meeting with those who are already known, provided that so far as practicable similar facilities or opportunities are offered to others who are identified later.

Elections are busy and tense times for the agents too, and it will help greatly if a proper professional relationship (and hopefully some mutual trust and confidence) can be established from the outset. It will also help in the election management process generally to clarify issues at the start, and avoid needless timetaking repetition. This will help you to get on with running the election, and them to get on with working to try and get their candidate(s) elected, with a minimum of distraction.

It is good practice to get the known agents together at the start of an election process – particularly those with a significant local or national profile. You can give them the forms, electoral register copies, and other information they will need, like where and when the issuing and opening of absent/postal votes will be; where and when the count will be; how to get count tickets (see chapter 16) from you; what the press and media arrangement will be; and so on. They can all ask questions, all hear the answers, and so reduce the scope for misunderstanding or later allegations that you treated one or other agent more or less helpfully.

There are fewer full time professional agents now than in earlier years but most usually make some form of contact with the returning officer before nominations close, so it is usually possible to have a reasonable meeting. Many part-time agents and secondees to the post find the task complex and difficult to understand - it really is a role learnt through experience.

Agents will appreciate knowing how to contact you and your Election Office quickly – perhaps using a telephone number different from the busier public ones. They will no doubt be quick to take up with you any issues of concern as their campaign continues, and an investment of time and courtesy at the outset should pay dividends later.

That is, after all, only good customer service.

But what are agents for? Essentially they manage the candidate's campaign for election, so freeing the candidate to undertake the actual campaigning. They will ordinarily direct events on the candidate's behalf, make contracts, publish election literature, submit the nomination and other required papers, and keep the financial records and control which will allow election accounts to be submitted to the returning officer both within the statutory period and within the prescribed expenditure limits (see chapter 23).

Achieving all that is of course their responsibility, not yours. Nevertheless, as already stated above, good and constructive co-operation (so long as you try to give it equally to all agents) will foster a mutually confident and professional relationship. Most agents are invariably grateful for all your help and understanding of their problems; after all, it is probable that you will work with them on more than one election!

CHAPTER 11
HANDLING THE NOMINATION PROCESS

Validly submitting the nomination papers is a key event of the electoral process – and a great relief – for agents and candidates. It is also important for the returning officer: the problems and ambiguities of nominations can generate a surprising degree of controversy and ill feeling.

A returning officer will no doubt have appointed a deputy (see chapter 4) for all or for certain purposes: no one can guarantee to be immediately available to receive nomination papers throughout all the possible office hours. The importance of being aware of nomination submissions cannot be over-stated: a wrong decision is going to lead to particularly difficult and expensive problems and challenges. A returning officer must either decide each case personally, or have full confidence in someone else validly appointed to do so. As to when a person is legally defined as becoming a candidate, see s 118A of the RPA 1983 added in by s 135 of the Political Parties, Elections and Referendums Act 2000.

A lot of legal cases have been generated over questions about signatures, capital letter, commonly used names like "Jack" for "John", and so on. The basic rules about nominations are set out in rules 6-17 of the Parliamentary Elections Rules (sch 1 to RPA 1983), and similarly elsewhere: e.g. rules 4-12 of SI 1986 No 2214 for local elections. As a general approach, you should be principled but not pedantic, and accurate but not academic or arcane. The aim is to accept nominations as valid if possible, but to respect the rules as process driven. The requirements are directive, not discretionary. Always remember, however, that your purpose as returning officer is to administer the process so that the electorate can make a choice between candidates and you are an enabler in this, not a preliminary selector. Thus, it is helpful to encourage the candidates/agents to arrive in good time during the nomination period to enable fresh papers to be submitted in the event of errors (most are well aware of this and try to avoid rushing into your office five minutes before the deadline).

Nomination papers need to be signed, as do consents to nomination. The former need to be holograph i.e. actually personally signed, on the paper presented. Fax or e-mail will not do: they would in any event arguably not have been "delivered" in the way the statutory rules mean.

It will be valid to accept a candidate's e-mailed or faxed consent to nomination if you are satisfied that the original has indeed been signed by the candidate, and you will normally be satisfied if there is no evidence to the contrary – even if you do not recognise the candidate's signature.

A deposit is required for Parliamentary elections (£500 – see rule 9) and European elections (£5,000 for individual candidates or party lists – see schedule 1 to SI 1999 No1214 modifying the Parliamentary rule 9). A nomination is not complete without receipt of the money. If that money does not arrive in cash, it must be in a form like a banker's draft which the returning officer can be sure will be honoured as good credit, and not drawn as a cheque (which could anyway be stopped) on a candidate, agent or political party. Note that the rule uses the term "legal tender" - this is not synonymous with "cash". The denominations of money that may be used as legal tender depend upon the amount to be paid. For the Parliamentary election (£500) only Bank of England notes or £1 coins are acceptable. The purpose of this is to stop publicity seeking candidates bringing in a wheelbarrow full of 10p pieces as, apparently, this has been tried!

Nominations close at a fixed time, which cannot be extended. If a nomination is not complete by 4pm on the closure day – for example because although a nomination paper has been properly completed and submitted a required deposit or candidate's consent has not been received – it cannot be completed later and the nomination must be rejected.

It is a good idea to be on the lookout just before closing time, and also just before the deadline within which any nominations validly submitted can be withdrawn. That will help to avoid allegations that someone was wrongly ruled out of time.

A sensible view must be taken of such borderlines. An agent or candidate need not be in the actual room where you check the submitted paper at withdrawal time (which for Parliamentary elections is the same time as closure of nominations) – it will be acceptable for them to have arrived in the reception area, and so present (so to speak) on your terms rather than theirs. But to be crossing the car park, or in the wrong building, or somewhere not within the scope of the address given for submission on the notice of election, is not acceptable and must be ruled out of time. Nomination papers are open to limited objections: see rule 15 of the Parliamentary Elections Rules. After the time for withdrawals has elapsed, a statement of persons nominated must be published: see rule 14.

A recent requirement in most elections is for candidates claiming political party membership to be able to stand as certified candidates for a political party registered under the Registration of Political Parties Act 1998, now being replaced by the Political Parties, Elections and Referendums Act 2000.

Finally, take note of the drafting of two rules in particular. First, the requirement in rule 7(4)(b) of the Parliamentary Elections Rules that on request a returning officer "shall prepare a nomination paper for signature". This simply means supplying a draft nomination paper with the election details filled in, so that the agent or candidate can fill in the personal details required and obtain the other subscriber or assentor counter-signatures required.

Secondly, be clear about the reasons for rejection of nomination papers under the rules: they are set out in rule 12(2) of the Parliamentary Elections Rules, plus rule 12(3A) inserted by rule 3(3) of sch 2 to the Registration of Political Parties Act 1998 in relation to political parties. The returning officer cannot bring in other considerations outside the scope of the procedural requirements involved, or look behind the papers and details present if, having checked the electoral register details given etc., there is no reason to do so. You are not expected to be a detective but a returning officer when checking papers. Unless there is an obvious error blatant on the face of the papers it is not your role to be the inquisitor of candidates and agents. The major texts record details of some of the problem cases, eg, the man who, wishing to stand as a candidate for a Parliamentary election, maintained his name was Margaret Hilda Thatcher and his address was 10 Downing Street, though in Peckham nor Westminster. Another candidate claimed his name as Mickey Mouse domiciled in Disneyland. This is a difficult topic with no clear answers, though the parties registration procedure has brought some further formality to the process and this is discussed below.

If at the end of the nomination period, or after the time limit for withdrawals, only one candidate stands duly nominated, then that person will be declared elected and of course there will be no poll. If no candidates stand nominated, the vacancy remains and the process has to begin again with a new notice of elections. Theoretically in the case of a Parliamentary election the writ would have to be "returned" blank. See para 17 (2) of the Parliamentary Elections Rules comprising sch 1 to the RPA 1983.

It is sensible for a returning officer to give a decision on the validity of a nomination paper or process as quickly as possible, even though the statutory deadline of closure of nominations may be some time away. Agents customarily submit more than one nomination paper for a candidate, particularly at Parliamentary elections, partly to be on the safe side and partly to encourage more subscribers who are perhaps key to their campaign effort. There is no harm in this: in the official record, the nomination paper first accepted and declared will stand.

The Registration of Political Parties Act 1998 introduced the concept of political parties as such into elections for the first time. The register of parties has previously been kept by the Register of Companies under the Companies Act 1985, but under s 23 of the Political Parties, Elections and Referendums Act 2000 is transferring to the new Electoral Commission. The new rule 14(5) of the Parliamentary Elections Rules, inserted by para 6 (9) of sch 21 to the Political Parties, Elections and Referendums Act 2000, requires the returning officer to send to the Electoral Commission a copy of the statement of persons nominated and, where candidates stand in the name of a registered party, a copy of the rule 6A certificate, on which see the next paragraph below and also para 41 of Home Office Circular RPA 436 dated 6 February 2001. As to this Act generally, see Home Office Circular 5/2001 dated 7 February 2001.

The register will not only contain the registered name of a given party, but also up to three emblems to be included on ballot papers. Most importantly for our purposes here, a candidate cannot use a description "which is likely to lead voters to associate the candidate with a registered political party" unless that description is authorised by a certificate from or on behalf of the party's registered nominating officer. (See rule 6A of the Parliamentary Elections Rules, inserted by para 2 of sch 2 to the 1998 Act).

The Registration of Political Parties (Prohibited Words and Expressions) Order 1998, SI No 2873, prevents political parties from registering using certain styles of naming or description. The register is public and to be maintained by the Electoral Commission. The register itself will be split between Great Britain and Northern Ireland and will be available to be consulted on the Electoral Commission's website, by returning officers; in the event of difficulty they should contact the Commission to confirm that a party is registered on the latest date for the publication of the notice of election.

For discussion and practical application of the 1998 Act, see the joint SOLACE/AEA publication *The Registration of Political Parties Act 1998: An Introductory Guide for Returning Officers* principally edited by David Monks (1999). There have been changes with the 2000 Act since that book was written and it is now worth noting the major difference, which is that to ensure the controls on party income and expenditure are binding on political parties a mechanism is introduced to bring parties within the registration scheme (previously voluntary). By virtue of s 22 of the Political Parties, Elections and Referendums Act 2000 nominations (except at parish and community council elections) must be accompanied by a certificate from a registered political party unless the description is "Independent", "the Speaker seeking re-election" or no description is given. Thus, the previous (and quite common descriptions) such as "Independent Conservative, Labour, Liberal, etc." are not valid and descriptions broadly along the lines of "Anti By-Pass Candidate" will also be unacceptable. There is also a new category of "minor party" for those involved solely in parish and community council elections. (An order is to be made to validate the Welsh equivalent of "Independent", which is "Annibynnol". Annex B to Home Office Circular RPA 436, published on 6 February 2001, reprints rules 6 and 6A of the Parliamentary Elections Rules as amended by the 2000 Act. Annex C following provides a useful question- and-answer briefing on candidates' descriptions.)

The Local Elections (Principal Areas)(Amendment) Rules 2001, SI No 81 have introduced related changes for local elections. Rule 4 amends rule 4A of sch 2 to the 1986 Rules (SI No 2214) in relation to registered parties, and rule 3 applies that in relation to a valid description of a nominated candidate (in addition to "Independent"). Rule 5 of the 2001

Rules allows a person to subscribe a nomination paper provided that they will be eligible to vote on polling day. Similar changes are made for parishes and communities in rules 3 and 4 of the Local Elections (Parishes and Communities) (Amendment) Rules 2001, SI No 80, amending SI 1986 No 2215. (These and other new changes are referred to in Home Office Circular RPA 437, dated 20 February 2001.)

If an election candidate dies before the result is declared, the poll is abandoned: see rule 60 of the Parliamentary Elections Rules.

CHAPTER 12
THE RETURNING OFFICER'S ROLE DURING THE CAMPAIGN

Returning officers and their staff are likely to be very busy during election periods. Is there anything else to be said about their roles at these times other than to speak of following through the statutory procedure?

We think there are two key areas, both about the returning officer's need for deliberate or positive impartiality. This situation is insufficiently described merely by referring to the statutory situation of being the holder of a politically restricted post.

First, it is quite likely that protagonists in an election campaign will seek to draw the returning officer into a kind of refereeing role, turning there for support in their eagerness or urgency to have someone else's conduct constrained or even declared unlawful. Candidates - and their agents - sometimes have difficulty in drawing the distinction between your role as returning officer and, say, chief executive of the council.

You are not the referee in the election. Strictly speaking, you have no more power or duty as returning officer than the various statutes and regulations give you. Nevertheless, it is often difficult to regard that as the last word.

Wrongdoing in elections can sometimes invalidate the process, depending on whether the breached requirements are mandatory or procedural: note that under s 23 (3) of the RPA 1983 for Parliamentary elections (and there are similar rules for other kinds of elections) procedural irregularities will not usually make an election invalid if the rules have substantially been met and the result has not been affected.[2] But wrongdoing can also amount to a criminal offence, and will certainly do so if there is a deliberate attempt to corrupt the fairness of the process or do something declared impermissible or unlawful. The wide variety of election offences are divided into corrupt practices and illegal practices, the broad distinction between which is about seriousness and degree of wilful intent (not unlike the classic criminal law distinction between felonies and misdemeanours, which subsisted until the passing of the Criminal Justice Act 1967).

---

[2] See also *Morgan v Simpson* [1975] Q.B.151, Lord Denning's judgement.

Of course, you have the same duty as any other citizen to act upon and report criminal offences, but there will be a greater expectation on you to do so as returning officer. If not you, protagonists often argue, who else will see fair play? And anyway, X is publishing scurrilous leaflets without saying who is printing and publishing them (s 110 of the RPA 1983, and see also s 143 of the Political Parties, Elections and Referendums Act 2000); Y is using a loud hailer close to the open doors of the polling station; and Z is spending more than allowed but laundering the bills.

This is where tact and robust common sense come in. These allegations are technically not your concern, but some response is seemingly required; often you may "have a quiet word", try to give constructive advice, or simply suggest that formal action might have to follow if present circumstances continue.

Sometimes candidates claim that their voters are being deterred by the most fanciful influences: it may be tempting to say airily "Do you think that could be true of your supporters? I thought you believed that they comprised the more sophisticated sector of the electorate?" But take care not to underestimate the strains and tensions of being up for election (and particularly re-election): many things will be said of which no more will be heard after polling day. So try to stay concerned but independent, ready to give friendly advice and warnings (so long as ready to do so similarly to all candidates), yet ready to report really serious wrongdoing if you do come across convincing evidence of it.

The second issue is about your continuing role in your substantive post – probably as chief executive, head of law and administration or similar. That continues and, although it is obviously politically restricted, it is (in a party politically controlled council) presumably work predominantly on behalf of the majority party or controlling administration.

This will not necessarily pose any problems, but in a vigorously contested election may produce some dilemmas. Suppose that the majority party uses its position to vote through resolutions and instructions which you (and perhaps other parties in particular) perceive as deliberately calculated to affect the election campaign and outcome?

Again, tact and caution will come in useful here, but there are three points in particular which it may be helpful to bear in mind.

The first is that you cannot validly or lawfully be asked to do anything which compromises your duty to the whole council, or your statutory duty to act in a politically restricted way as s 2 of the Local Government and Housing Act 1989 requires. We do not have to assume corruption or a criminal act by someone else to envisage something compromising arising for you. You must be polite but firm about any such situation, which could potentially involve professional misconduct.

The second point is about capacity. You are wearing two hats, one as (deputy) returning officer, and one as whatever your main post is. They are statutorily separate and, up to a point, you can act separately and distinctly. There is, of course, still some danger from the perception of others, or the possibility that your stance and conduct in one position is such as to cast a shadow across the other and jeopardise the reality of being seen to act fairly and without bias (say, for example, if you were publishing a district council viewpoint about a matter currently the subject of a parish poll you were required to conduct). Nevertheless, with a judicious approach you should hopefully be able to fulfil a regular role as an advocate of, and champion for, your council's – and hence probably its majority group's – interests without jeopardising the proper conduct of your role in the election process.

The third point is about expenses. No one should forget the rules about spending money to try to procure the election of a given candidate, and bringing that into account. A reminder might be timely to anyone seeking by surrogate means effectively to deploy resources which would take a given campaign's expenditure beyond the lawful limits.

You may also be approached about campaigning facilities. Sections 95 and 96 of the RPA 1983 provide for Parliamentary and local election candidates to have free access to certain schools and meeting rooms for election meetings – in effect the same kind of definition as referred to in chapter 6 as able to be requisitioned by returning officers for polling stations. "Free" means free of any booking or hiring fee – the costs of heating, lighting and cleaning etc. still have to be paid: ss 95 (4) and 96 (4).

CHAPTER 13

POLL CARDS

Poll cards are simply the written communications sent to individual electors to tell them where and when they can vote at a particular election. They are required for most elections: the rules are prescribed in rule 28 of the Parliamentary Elections Rules (sch 1 to RPA 1983), and rule 22 of the Local Elections (Principal Areas) Rules 1986 SI No 2214. For European elections the Parliamentary rule is modified by sch 1 to the European Parliamentary Elections Regulations 1999, SI No 1214, and for the Welsh Assembly see rule 33 of sch 5 to the National Assembly for Wales (Representation of the People) Order 1999, SI No 450.

Poll cards do not include details of the candidates standing. They can include maps of polling stations, but even with today's technology mapping is still quite costly compared with basic cards. It is also likely that, to provide identifiable maps which most electors can use, such poll cards may need to be larger, at perhaps A5 sizes, than the usual postcard size customarily used. Use of maps on cards may incur Ordnance Survey fees. Some authorities now produce poll cards which also "double up" as applications for postal votes, once signed and returned to the returning officer; clearly a rapid delivery system is required if this is to be successful.

The RPR 2001, SI No 341 (reg 9) now prescribes the form of poll cards for Parliamentary elections (form A in sch 3, not to be confused with the Form A for pre-2001 electoral register canvassing which was delivered to every household). This appears not to extend to local elections but the format would be very similar. For combined elections (see chapter 24) it is possible to send out separate cards, but it is much more usual to have a combined version to take advantage of the resultant cost savings.

It is usual to send out poll cards as quickly as possible after the statement of persons nominated has been published. Inevitably that means that some people who apply for absent voters, particularly under the late applications procedure, will receive poll cards.

It is a common misconception that intending voters need to bring their poll cards to identify themselves at the polling stations, but this is not so. Voters are identified by the statutory questions, which the polling staff put. Poll cards need not be sent to people who have applied for absent voters (see chapter 14).

Poll cards are required for all main elections, but they are not statutorily required for parish or community council elections, although those councils can ask for poll cards to be issued if they pay the cost; see rule 22 of the Local Elections (Parishes and Communities) Rules 1986, SI No 2215. Home Office Circular RPA 264 dated 10 December 1982 reminded returning officers that poll cards could in turn remind voters that polls are being taken together where district and parish or Welsh equivalent elections are being combined.

It is an offence to distribute imitation poll cards calculated to deceive: see s 94 of the RPA 1983. This can sometimes cause problems as over zealous agents occasionally produce party literature that copies poll cards or ballot papers exhorting the voter to support their candidate(s).

CHAPTER 14

ABSENT VOTES

There are two kinds of absent votes – postal votes, and proxy votes. In 2001 the rules have been changed substantially and liberalised, particularly in respect of allowing postal votes on demand. The rules are now set out in sch 4 of the RPA 2000, parts IV and V of the RPR 2001. The old ideas of having to claim infirmity or absence on business have been scrapped and postal voting applications need not contain any reason now. They may be granted for definite or indefinite periods or a particular election. The notice of election must set out the date by which applications must be received. Prescribed reasons are still required for proxy votes, whether permanent or for a given election. A proxy vote can be exercised by post on demand.

Strangely, candidates and election agents are now no longer entitled to be present when absent votes are prepared for despatch. They are able, however, to attend when they are opened, so notice must accordingly be given of these occasions (more than one, almost certainly) and times. It will also be helpful to say in advance when absent votes will be despatched, even though the right to be present has been abolished, as candidates and agents will find that information useful for their campaigning.

The paperwork for the absent vote procedure is demanding and bureaucratic, even under the new approach: the requirements for preparing absent votes for despatch take time to complete and should not be under-estimated. Indeed, it is highly likely that postal voting on demand will lead to a considerable increase in postal votes, particularly in Parliamentary elections. Moreover, the new rules extend the deadline for receipt of applications (see rule 56 of RPR 2001) and returning officers should seriously consider employing extra staff now to cope with this prospective increase in workload. Close liaison with local postal staff is also essential - they must clearly understand the deadlines of the electoral timetable (examples in appendices 2 and 3). A new rule 19 on the issuing of postal votes in local elections has been substituted into sch 2 to the Local Elections (Principal Areas) Rules 1986, SI No 2214, by SI 2001 No 81, para 7. Rule 11 of SI 2001 No 80 makes a similar change for parishes and communities, amending sch 2 to SI 1986 No 2215, rule 39 (3).

Interestingly, it is now possible to use council staff to deliver postal ballots, or a commercial delivery firm. Again, there is no longer a restriction that addresses for postal ballot papers must be within the United Kingdom. Return postage is to be prepaid for those sent to United Kingdom addresses only.

Similarly it is easy for those voting to make mistakes over the requirements to certify identity, etc. and the opportunities for time taking and uncertainty are considerable.

Proxy voting requirements have not been similarly changed and there are still prescribed grounds for applications (eg physical incapacity, service voter, attendance on a course, etc.). An elector cannot have more than one proxy at once, even if more than one constituency is involved: see s 8 (2) of the RPA 1985 (now becoming para 6 (2) of sch 4 to the RPA 2000). To be a proxy voter, a person must be eighteen, not subject to any legal incapacity, and be from either the Commonwealth or the Republic of Ireland. Except in specified family relationship, a person cannot be a proxy for more than two electors in the same parliamentary constituency or electoral area (i.e. district, borough or parish etc. – it does not mean ward or electoral division): see s 8 (5) of the RPA 1985 (now becoming para 6 (6) of sch 4 to the RPA 2000) and S 203 (1) of the RPA 1983. Most returning officers do not try positively to check for compliance with this limit and only react to it if obliged to do so by its coming obviously to their attention. There is a risk otherwise that an unwilling and quite genuine absent vote applicant might be turned down because unknown to them their proxy has agreed to act in more cases than permitted. Arguably if there is excess, the first two only (plus any permitted family situations) will be valid.

There are some further changes (RPR 2001) in the notification to applicants for proxy votes by the electoral registration officer. Notification of allowance of postal votes continues to be required only "where practicable" (reg 57 (1), RPR 2001). During the busy election period, immediately before the deadlines for receipt of such applications (see timetables, appendices 2 and 3) it is considered futile to issue such notices – no one is looking for extra tasks at this juncture! However, the same dispensation for notification of allowance of proxy votes has been removed (reg 57(2), RPR 2001). Thus, at all times, however, busy, it is necessary to confirm to the applicant elector the name, address and duration of the proxy appointment. There have been, at some elections, allegations of abuse of proxy votes, e.g. encouraging elderly and infirm people (often in local authority care) to sign blank forms with vague references to postal (ie personal) voting, but then completing the proxy application later. This change seeks to eliminate such malpractice.

For further discussion and explanation see the joint AEA/SOLACE publication *The Representation of the People Act 2000 and the Representation of the People Regulations 2001: Interpretation, Guidance and Good Practice* edited by John Owen (January 2001).

CHAPTER 15
POLLING AGENTS AND TELLERS

Polling agents are provided for in rule 30 of the Parliamentary Elections Rules (sch 1 to the RPA 1983). Before polling starts, candidates can appoint polling agents "for the purpose of detecting personation" (voting in person - or by post - as some other person, whether that other person is living, dead or fictitious). There is no limit on the number who can be appointed, and they can be paid or unpaid, but of course candidates are responsible for the actions of their agents. Returning officers must be notified of the names and addresses of those appointed "not later than the second day" (ie valid timetable days) "before the day of the poll:" rule 30 (3).

There is, it seems, in certain places, an increasing tendency to appoint polling agents today, even if personation is not a prevalent problem. The advantage to candidates (and the agents) is that polling agents are allowed to be present inside the polling stations themselves. Unless the returning officer allows a greater number by notice, four is the maximum number of polling agents allowed at a particular polling station, and if more than four have been appointed the returning officer must decide which four are allowed by lot. A person can be a polling agent for more than one candidate, and candidates can be their own polling agents in effect: see rule 24 (2), (3) and (10), for instance, of sch 2 to the Local Elections (Principal Areas) Rules 1986, SI No 2214. Acting as their own polling agent will not increase the total allowed in a given polling station above four, but candidates are entitled to be present there anyway – see rule 26 (1) (a).

Polling agents must not interfere with voters or the process of their voting. They can, however, require under rule 35 that the formal questions to voters or proxies be put by the presiding officer; but they are not permitted directly to put them themselves. They must be notified of, and abide by, the requirements of secrecy: rule 31(a).

The rules on polling agents are the same in their application to all forms of elections (though in a referendum or parish or community poll, there are no candidates to appoint them even though personation is equally a possibility). They can be appointed for parish and community council elections as for other kinds and have the same rights – see the Local Elections (Parishes and Communities) Rules 1986, SI No 2215, sch 2, rules 26 (1) (b) and 29.

Whereas polling agents have a statutory, if incidental, role to play, tellers do not. They are entirely informal appointments, typically asked to stand outside polling stations asking voters for their electoral register numbers. Tellers will typically tend to encroach into the polling station entrance if not discouraged, and they must be politely but firmly controlled. Many voters find them intrusive, and are unsympathetic to the general aim of trying to record who has been to vote. Tellers were the subject of Home Office Circular RPA 359 dated 3 December 1991, incorporating useful guidance for returning officers. It is a matter of some regret that political parties do not encourage their staff to take more notice of the guidance code and seek to control "aggressive telling".

CHAPTER 16

PLANNING THE COUNT

An election count is a major event in itself. Other than for some by-elections, it may involve the possible presence of some hundreds of people. Counts generally take place at night, at the end of an already long and probably physically demanding day. Tension is often high: candidates, agents and supporters have a lot at stake, and so does the returning officer. The whole exercise is very public and visible: if it goes wrong there is likely to be serious embarrassment at least, escalating, possibly, to very expensive High Court litigation in the more extreme situations.

So a checklist of things to consider may be helpful – particularly if you plan to use premises not used for counts before.

(i) The timing of the count. Most counts take place at night, but it is demanding (particularly in these days of the Working Time Directive) to start a count at 10pm after polling for fifteen hours. Separate counting staff can be used, but for you and certain key staff very long hours may be inevitable. At combined polls (eg as on 1 May 1997) many of you will be back the next day after only a brief rest.

(ii) Booking the venue. Most election dates are predictable, and places big enough to hold counts are often in short supply. Book as far ahead as you can. As with polling stations (see chapter 6), you can requisition some kinds of premises. If the Home Office is paying, they will question using a private hall at a commercial rate if you could have used a council leisure centre at actual cost (see also chapter 22).

(iii) Is the venue suitable? Think this through carefully, using squared paper or floor measurement if necessary. Is the main room big enough? Is it secure from outside view, which could compromise confidentiality? Can you cope with excited groups crowding round particular areas? Is there circulation space to check people in securely but quickly? Can you put press and media somewhere? Does the building have adequate communications including a private direct line you can use yourself? Can you yourself get into the middle, round the tables etc.? Can you put people somewhere safe and under cover (and keep tabs on them) if you have to evacuate for a bomb threat or the fire alarm goes off?

Then there are other organisational matters. Suppose that 90% of your polling station presiding officers arrive over a twenty-minute peak period. Can they get in by car quickly, park, deliver the ballot box, the ballot paper account, and all their "clobber" quickly? They're tired: they just want to go home. Can you count them in easily? Have you plenty of help to take their deliveries to the right places systematically? Will you pile all those plastic sacks in a big heap or in a proper order, so that when you have to look for some sack an hour later you can find it quickly? Is there enough space to handle and decide allegedly spoilt votes properly? Is there somewhere you personally can sit down (it's going to be a long night...)? Should you give your staff some refreshment facilities?

Some returning officers try to produce a flow chart to show the progress of ballot boxes through the process; checking in, storage pending emptying, being counted, stored when empty, eventual checking out and back to the depot (or wherever). This flow has not got to be impeded so you need to think carefully about, for example, whether or not to have a public gallery. Space usually dictates, but there are some people who enjoy the tension of the count and dress especially for the occasion. They should have separate points of entrance and egress in the hall, particularly if patronising the bar (see (vii) below).

(iv) What media arrangements are necessary? Press and public relations staff can be invaluable at this time, shielding you from needless distraction. Modern technology make it less physically demanding than once it was, but it is still necessary to make sure that they are covering your event and not expecting it to be conducted for their benefit. At the same time, it is not sensible to be unhelpful or rigid in your approach: they have a job to do too, and this is a television age. Responsible broadcasters are not trying to breach the obligations of secrecy: they just want to get the result out first and as fast as possible, and to interview the winner in particular afterwards.

In "high profile" counts (such as the Prime Minister's constituency) particular effort needs to be made with the media (over 250 turned up at Huntingdon in 1997 from all over the world with all their considerable paraphernalia) and it is worthwhile having early briefing meetings with them. Some can be unreasonable - eg, wanting to install hidden ceiling cameras "to observe body language" (allegedly) - and they should be resisted firmly but politely. You are in charge as returning officer with a significant task to achieve and it is not entertainment for the masses whatever television producers might think. It is reasonable to charge the media for their use of electricity, premises, etc.

(v) What security arrangements are necessary? Take police advice on the security alert situation for the count, and what cover you need in the event of public disorder. Tempers can fray very easily at the end of a long night, especially if people have been in the bar while you and your staff were completing the verification! If not yourself, have someone at hand who knows the building's systems (and how to get at them) very well.

Similarly, with high profile counts expect considerable disruption in the week preceding polling day with Special Branch much in evidence searching drains, running names through computers, etc. At Huntingdon in 1997 there were armed police (some more obvious than others) and all ballot boxes coming into the hall were "sniffed" by police dogs. Clearly, all this takes time and needs to be integrated into your arrangements.

(vi) Issuing admission tickets. The various rules prescribe who is entitled by law to be present at a count: see for example rule 44 (2) of the Parliamentary Elections Rules in sch 1 to the RPA 1983, and rules 38 (2) of both the Local Elections (Principal Areas) and (Parishes and Communities) Rules 1986, SI Nos 2214 and 2215 respectively (but note that the latter does not include election agents, as they are not provided for in the parish and community election process). The rest need your permission; under the rules 44 (3) and 38 (3) respectively; everyone will need tickets. Ensure that agents know in advance how many they can have (see chapter 18) and what arrangements you will be making (probably at the last minute) to get them distributed via the agents or whatever. (Carry a few spares in your pocket just in case.)

(vii) Bar facilities. There is no formal objection to there being bar facilities at a count venue, but of course they must be entirely separate from the spaces required for the count access and progress. It is a matter of personal judgement whether or not to have a bar and practice varies considerably. Many returning officers feel it is not a necessary part of the process and, often, the political parties repair to other premises after the count has finished. Whether to apply for any extension, which may be necessary, is a matter of judgement!

Take note of local practice and expectations and the practicalities. In a rural or inner city area, getting counting staff for late night work may be particularly hard. On the other hand, deferring counting to the following day (with the attendant problems of overnight ballot box security) may make many would-be counting staff (from banks, for example) unavailable. Agents and candidates generally press for a night count and this is usual practice in the United Kingdom. Some constituencies - e.g. in Western Scotland, with islands - count the next day as a matter of course because of the time it takes for all the boxes to be brought into a central point. What matters ultimately is not a quick result but a well-ordered and correct result. That is your over-riding duty, regardless of pressures from candidates or media. And the decision is one for you to make personally, not for your employing authority.

At the busiest elections it may help and is common practice if a trusted colleague (often one of your deputy returning officers) takes a particular lead for you on count planning and logistics. There is too much to leave to the last minute.

As to actually conducting the count, see chapter 18.

CHAPTER 17

ON POLLING DAY

Whether it's a local election from 8am – 9pm or a Parliamentary or European from 7am – 10pm, polling day is long.

Polling station staff should have a direct telephone line number on which to contact your election office. Almost inevitably there will be the usual crop of oversleeping caretakers or staff, locked gates, "no shows", no heating or power, no ballot paper account or whatever.

How you respond quickly depends on the nature of the problem and the area. Mobile telephones help a lot today – so does carrying a few useful spares around in the car. Some heavy-duty gaffer tape will prove invaluable if it's wet and windy and some of the posters won't stay up.

Pacing yourself and your key helpers is vital. The hot meal, the shower, the few minutes of fresh air – whatever works best for you will prove invaluable late at night when you've been up for eighteen hours and still need to work calmly and effectively with your usual sense of judgement.

Even if you have organised several "openings" beforehand still allow adequate time to open the postal votes (allowing the rights of inspection, of course). Check the Town Hall letterbox at 9.01 or 10.01pm in case a vote has been hand-delivered at the last minute. It is now possible to return postal votes to any polling station, though, in logic, this seems to defeat the original purpose - see RP Regulations 2001, rule 79 and rule 39 (3) of sch 2 to the Local Elections (Principal Areas) Rules 1986, SI No 2214, substituted by rule 12 of SI 2001 No 81. We suggest you drink no alcohol whatsoever that day, so that no allegations of, or opportunities for, mischief can arise.

Wear sober clothing, and avoid obvious colours that could be alleged to be tacit signals of party support.

It is a good idea to go out yourself to visit a few polling stations as soon as polling opens, particularly including any problem cases. It gives you a feel for the day, and when someone rings up to complain about what's happening at St Joseph's Community Centre it's helpful to be able to say that you've been out and about a bit – even if not to that particular location. Most returning officers appoint a number of experienced staff (probably your deputies) to tour round an allocated number of stations during the day - this is particularly helpful in the larger rural districts. It is now recognised Home Office practice that they will meet the reasonable costs of polling station inspectors for Parliamentary elections.

Good communications are vital on polling day – if a problem arises time is short and people want to speak to you quickly. Similarly you have little time to respond. Self-evidently all these impressions will contribute much to an overall opinion about whether the whole process is well under control. At the same time lots of issues which seem big and noisy on polling day fade in the calmer climate of the morrow and are not pursued.

The stories of what returning officers find at polling stations are now the stuff of legend and memoirs - staff who are either missing or sunbathing. Aerobic classes taking place in the school hall with the polling table being pushed to one side...the polling station staff openly watching Eastenders on television... It is all part of being a returning officer . . .

CHAPTER 18

CONDUCTING THE COUNT

Plainly the thoroughness and outcome of your planning (see chapter 16) will predicate the conduct of the count itself. The factors that need to be thought about in forward planning need not be repeated here.

The big counts – particularly on general election night – are part of the traditional British election scene, and often seem as much pieces of theatre as repetitive, old-fashioned counting. However much we now talk about consulting the public and send them our well-turned community strategies, here with the aid of radio, television and the internet we can witness for ourselves the verdicts of the people of Blyth, Birmingham and Bognor on the government of the day: a win here, a lost deposit or someone dressed as a chicken there. Being part of this sort of atmosphere helps attract the numbers of staff you need, and provides a burst of adrenalin to offset the fatigue of a long day. But it also holds the dangers of being so visibly on public show in your direction and management of events, when tensions are high and tired people with much at stake behave and react differently from the individuals you normally know.

Try to get counting staff in place in good time, keeping a reserve or two in case of need. Consider if you need a "runner" – a helper with no other duties who can respond immediately to some need arising which would distract you or the regular staff.

Mobile telephones are a nuisance at counts – they can be carried, but insist they be switched off, and be firm with anyone seen using one in the room(s) where the actual counting is taking place – the potential for breach, or perceived breach, of the secrecy requirement is obvious.

Keep an eye on the layout you planned (see chapter 16). It's easy for a ballot box to be accidentally put on the wrong pile unopened if your handling process doesn't try to make that unlikely. Getting this count right is an acutely personal responsibility, but you have to be dependent on others. Brief them well; guard against obvious mistakes; but then show trust in them too.

How many counting assistants can you employ? Naturally this depends on how large the counting task to be done, your view on the probability of a very high or low turnout, and so on. You will also need an additional number of counting supervisors and overall help at the centre where you and others will be directing operations, checking ballot papers accounts and matching them with verified totals from the individual ballot boxes, and later deciding on allegedly spoilt votes, and so on. If the election costs are to be recharged or recovered from elsewhere, particularly the Home Office, the costs of conducting the count will have to be contained within the clerical pool and heading allowed (see chapter 20).

The number of counting assistants, i.e. actual counters at the tables, not including the supervisory or central staff, determines by law the minimum number of counting agents you must allow the candidates to have present. Counting agents are also loosely called "scrutineers".

Rule 30 (2) of the Parliamentary Elections Rules, sch 1 to the RPA 1983, provides that the returning officer must afford each candidate the same number of counting agents, and that number "shall not (except in special circumstances) be less than the number obtained by dividing the number of clerks employed on the counting by the number of candidates".

If there are several candidates, and some with few supporters compared with the candidates of nationally known political parties, such candidates may not need or be able to take up their quota of places. What is required is equality of opportunity, not of outcome, so once the deadline for appointing counting agents has passed (not later than the second election timetable day before the poll – see rule 30 (3)), any untaken allocation of places can be offered even-handedly to other candidates (most mainstream parties usually take their full allocation, however). This is done under the returning officer's general discretion in the last words of rule 44 (1), as technically it is then too late for original regular appointments (although appointment has to be simply "before the commencement of the poll" (rule 30 (1)). Written notice of appointments has been given earlier under rule 30 (3).

Once you have a provisional result, you should consult the election agents on the figures. In practice candidates are often present too, but your formal dealings are with the agents they have appointed. The agents should have a chance to check the figures, and express a view on whether they accept the outcome from an arithmetical or formal standpoint.

Checking that the figures add up will be easier if they already know the turnout percentage. There is no objection to giving this out within the count room (ie publicly to those present, but not broadcast outside the count). At the European elections of 1999 when verification mainly took place on polling day, Thursday 10 June, but counting on the following Sunday 13 June, it was decided that verification information per Parliamentary constituency could be made available. At that stage it can compromise neither the eventual outcome nor the personal secrecy of the poll.

What about re-counts? This is in the returning officer's sole discretion, but agents need to understand your decision and reasoning. Unless it is manifestly perverse, one request for a recount is easily granted. Subsequent requests depend on the circumstances. Totals need not be exactly the same if differences are minor and wholly inconsequential. It may be appropriate to recount to ascertain whether or not a deposit is lost, even if the main outcome is clear beyond doubt. A result should not be finally declared without warning to the agents, even if one of them is still disputing it.

The actual declaration should be conducted openly and visibly and audibly: sometimes candidates wish to gather behind the declarer, or television producers want a nod before you start. All of this is down to common sense, and recognition that this is an event of considerable public interest, the image of which you want to foster, not worsen.

It is not necessary to say "I the undersigned" in the ponderous way of municipal legend. Read the result in a sensible but objective way – and consider giving a returning officer in a Parliamentary election a prepared text to read so that they do not have to wrestle with a stylised formal public notice kind of declaration. Speeches from candidates generally follow and it must be fairly said that, virtually as a matter of course, they all remember to thank the returning officer and staff for their hard work. Again, as to length of speeches, order, etc. much of this is down to common sense with the victor always speaking first. In list elections (eg the European election of 1999) some constituencies had 50 or 60 candidates and it was simply impossible for them all to speak. It is best to come to an understanding with agents well prior to the actual declaration.

Counting staff should not be released until you are sure you are ready to declare. The count has to be continuous, but rule 30 (6) does give authority to agree with the agents that the hours between 7pm and the following 9am can be excluded. Sometimes sheer fatigue on everyone's part forces a pause after three recounts or whatever: securing the count room in a sealed state at this point is vital so that events can resume later without allegations of impropriety while the candidates and counting agents were absent.

Earlier in this chapter we have referred to the Parliamentary Elections Rules, but there are equivalents elsewhere for other kinds of elections: see for instance rules 24 (4) of both the Local Elections (Principal Areas) Rules 1986, SI No 2214, and the Local Elections (Parishes and Communities) Rules 1986, SI No 2215. Mayor of London and London Assembly elections are made local elections but with some modifications not relevant here: see s 17 of, and sch 3 to, the Greater London Authority Act 1999. See also on the Welsh Assembly s 11 of the Government of Wales Act 1998 and paras 35 (2) – (15) of sch 5 and para 9 of Part II of sch 4 to the National Assembly for Wales (Representation of the People) Order 1999, SI No 450.

At a local election for which you are the proper officer to accept the declaration of acceptance of office (see s 83 (1) of the Local Government Act 1972), it is helpful to have the declaration forms or book written up as far as possible beforehand so that you can insert the required full names and signatures.

Doing that will save chasing people later, though many still follow this practice. It will also reduce the problems of queuing when the bulk of the individual results are declared over a short space of time.

At elections for which deposits are required, be ready to return deposits, which have not been forfeited – or else do it the following day, which is what the law requires (see rule 53 of the Parliamentary Elections Rules, sch 1 to the RPA 1983).

At general Parliamentary elections it is your responsibility to return the writ as acting returning officer, unless the returning officer elects to do so (see section B, chapter 4). The writ must be endorsed with the successful candidate's full name and title (such as Rt Hon) for the Clerk of the Crown (who receives the writ) takes this for entry into his register at the Crown Office. The details given in the nomination papers will not necessarily suffice (where forenames, for instance, may be abbreviated) so it is, again, worthwhile checking with the actual victor or their agent. The returning officer must sign the writ personally and it is worthwhile taking a photocopy before dispatch. There is a special envelope provided for the post and it should reach the Clerk of the Crown before midnight on the Sunday following the election. Finally with regard to the return of the writ, you are usually instructed to write your home/holiday (!) telephone number by your name in case the Clerk's office wants to speak to you urgently, presumably because they cannot read your writing - so make it legible!

So how long should all this take? Why do some counts take just over an hour and some seven hours or even longer? Clearly, the time taken to garner in all the ballot boxes varies between compact city areas and large rural constituencies. Without doubt, however, there are certain constituencies where substantial short-cuts are taken with established procedure in an effort to be the first result declared. Such short cuts could never be recommended in any text dealing with running elections and, as we pointed out at the end of chapter 16, an accurate result is the aim, not a mistaken outcome however rapidly achieved. Indeed, it is well worth taking another twenty minutes or so checking the figures, even at 2.30/3 am, to complete the task properly rather than face the prospect of an election petition. There are enough pitfalls in the count process without needlessly adding a time problem; moreover, civic pride and kudos in declaring the first result on live television will soon dissipate in the recriminations of petition litigation.

CHAPTER 19
WHEN THE ELECTION IS OVER

Once the election is over there is much mopping up to do, despite the probable feeling of fatigue and anti-climax which follows a period of intense activity or tension.

A priority is the payment of all election staff, together with their expenses. So too is getting in, and then paying, the invoices for room and equipment hire and so on. The results have to be posted, and earlier posters, like notices of election and notices of poll, taken down.

If deposits are involved and have not been forfeited, they must be returned as soon as practicable after the counting is completed. Ordinarily return by "not later than the next day" is required – see rule 53 of the Parliamentary Elections Rules, sch 1 to the RPA 1983. Candidates/agents will take your cheque, though some returning officers retain banker's drafts in situ in their safes and return these; this avoids a fee from the bank. Forfeited deposits should be forwarded within fourteen days to the Home Office Elections Unit at Liverpool - again, they will take acting returning officer cheques.

It is a good idea to remind agents of the date by which they need to file returns of candidates' expenses with you. Councillors also need to be reminded of the rules about donations to them contained in s 7 of, and sch 7 to, Political Parties, Elections and Referendums Act 2000.

The law helps to move things along by providing (with equivalent provisions for other kinds of elections) in s 78 of the RPA 1983 that claims against candidate or agents not sent to the relevant agent within 21 days of the day of declaration of the result "shall be barred and not paid". (Section 79 provides disputed claims procedure.)

Returns are due in to the returning officer within 35 days of the day of declaration under s 81, to be accompanied by a declaration as required by s 82 of, and sch 3 to, the RPA 1983. The returning officer must publish a notice within 10 days of the time allowed for receiving expenses returns, advertising facilities for inspection (or indeed default if no return has been received), and must copy the notice to each of the election agents. Notices must be published in at least two newspapers circulating in the constituency. Returns are open to inspection for two years: see ss 88 – 89 of the RPA 1983. (As to the level of permitted expenses, see s 76 of the 1983 Act.) Once again these requirements are essentially structured in the same way for elections, but there are some differences in particular cases – see for example the Secretary of State's power to vary permitted expense levels in para 50 of the National Assembly for Wales (Representation of the People) Order 1999, SI No 450.

The duty is to receive returns, not prepare them or advise upon their content; try to avoid favouring some candidates with your comments and assistance by maintaining a neutral role.

Section 87A of the RPA 1983, inserted by the Political Parties, Elections and Referendums Act 2000, requires the returning officer at a Parliamentary or Mayor of London election to send to the Electoral Commission "as soon as reasonably practicable" a copy of any return or declaration received under sections 75, 81 or 82 of the 1983 Act. See also para 39 of Home Office Circular RPA 436 dated 6 February 2001.

Note that when a returning officer passes to a local authority proper officer the election documents after a count is completed, they must be retained for six months: see rules 46–48 of both the Local Elections (Principal Areas) Rules 1986, SI No 2214 and the Local Elections (Parishes and Communities) Rules 1986, SI No 2115.

As to the returning officer's personal accounts, see chapter 22.

CHAPTER 20
ELECTION FEES AND STAFF PAYMENTS

For national elections, fees are prescribed on a fixed scale. The scale is updated, usually just before General Elections, and while the levels are not agreed by negotiation, SOLACE/ALACE/AEA usually have an opportunity to make representations to the Home Office before the Secretary of State seeks Parliamentary approval through the statutory instrument procedure.

For local elections the fees scales and payments or costs limits are set by the local authority concerned which employs the returning officer. There is a range of local discretion, as is the case with local authority pay rates generally. This is usually done on a county basis so local authorities have the same fees as in neighbouring areas and do not compete with one another for staff. (London has special weighting.)

Fee orders have a basic division into fees payable to the returning officer personally, and sums made available to the returning officer to defray the costs of running the election. An acting returning officer does not simply receive a set flat fee for a Parliamentary election (the formal returning officer receives no fee at all). Elements of the process vary accordingly to constituency size, number of absent votes involved, and so on. Nevertheless the scales are today somewhat old fashioned in paying separately for different aspects of the process. Efforts have been made by SOLACE/ALACE/AEA to have the whole system of fees simplified but without any notable success to date; these discussions continue with the Home Office Elections Unit staff. Note that reductions in returning officer fees are made for multiple constituencies.

The current Parliamentary fee order is the Parliamentary Elections (Returning Officers' Charges) Order 1997, SI No 1034, due to be uprated for inspection ahead of the next general election. Part A of that Order prescribes the (acting) returning officer's personal fees; the rest of the Order is further subdivided into returning officer's costs "for which maximum recoverable amounts are specified" (Part B) and those for which there is no maximum specified (Part C), essentially including costs which are variable for local conditions like supplies, services and travelling expenses.

The equivalent fee orders for European and Welsh Assembly elections are currently the European Parliamentary Elections (Returning Officers'

Charges) Order 1999, SI No 1378, the European Parliamentary Elections (Local Returning Officers' Charges) Order 1999, SI No 1377 and the National Assembly for Wales (Returning Officers' Charges) Order 1999, SI No 942.

The amount available to pay for your general help – that is, administration and associated overheads separate from fixed amount expenditures, is generally referred to as the "clerical pool". It should be sufficient to pay for what is required, but like any other budget situation the expenditure needs to be properly estimated beforehand and monitored. The returning officer will be personally liable for any excessive or improper expenditure. (See also chapter 22.)

Election staff do not receive huge sums (tax deducted by returning officer at source) so it is only fair not to delay their payment. Returning officers use various methods of financial administration. To sign literally hundreds of cheques personally is very time consuming. It is possible to authorise a couple of deputies to do this, but it is also possible to use the finance department to make payments out of the election account by requisition; this latter process can also complement any later audit. It is simply not possible to know, as returning officer, every payment that is made but, as this is your personal responsibility, it is sensible to have some level of general oversight and know, at least, where the larger personal payments occur in the accounts. Again, difficulties in recruiting staff can only be reduced if payment levels are increased, and the professional societies continue to press this legitimate claim.

Chapter 4 refers to which fees received by returning officers are pensionable and which not.

CHAPTER 21
ELECTION PETITIONS

If an election process or decision is to be questioned while the course of that process continues, such a challenge will have to be made by way of judicial review, probably seeking a declaration or otherwise invalidating a decision.

Once the result of an election has been declared, if it is to be questioned the procedure will be by way of election petition.

At a Parliamentary election, the petition can be prescribed by either a voter or a candidate or claimed candidate. The respondent is either the candidate declared elected or, if the conduct of the returning officer is impugned, the returning officer.

The detailed procedure is the object of Part III of the RPA 1983, ss 136 – 157 of which provides the procedure on all election petitions. Twenty-one days after return of the writ is the normal time limit for presenting petitions: s 122 (1) of the RPA 1983. It is not necessary to review that procedure in detail here: see the Election Petition Rules 1960, SI No 543, as amended by SIs 1985 No 1278 and SI 1999 No 1352. The most recent Parliamentary election petition involved the May 1997 general election at Winchester. As to special cases to be determined by the High Court, see s 146.

The Parliamentary election procedures apply similarly, apart from one or two modifications, to the European Parliament and the Welsh Assembly. See in the first case the Special European Parliamentary Election Petition Rules 1979, SI No 521 (as amended by SIs 1998 No 557 and 1999 No 1398); in the case of Wales see Part IV of the National Assembly for Wales (Representation of the People) Order 1999, SI No 450.

Local government election petitions share much of the same statutory background under ss 127 – 128 of the RPA 1983. Apart from candidates or claimed candidates, however, four local government electors, not just one as in the earlier cases, are necessary: s 128 (1). The time limit is again 21 days "after the day on which the election was held" (s 129 (1)), i.e. not the day of declaration of the result.

With regard to mayoral referendums similar provisions will be set out in reg 19 of the draft Local Authorities (Conduct of Referendums)

(England) Regulations 2001, broadly substituting "referendum petition" in place of "election petition".

Needless to say, if a petition results in action in the High Court it is an immensely serious situation with considerable ramifications - hence the need for insurance. High Court litigation can easily run bills up to six figures and it is simply essential to take advice at an early stage on such matters. Fortunately, such petitions are rare, but never to be ignored!

CHAPTER 22
THE RETURNING OFFICER'S ACCOUNTS

We have referred in chapters 19 and 20 to paying the bills, paying the staff and yourself, and to settling the election accounts generally and reclaiming the cost if the expense is borne by the Home Office or elsewhere. How should a returning officer or equivalent hold money paid to him or her for defraying the costs of running the election?

Such monies belong, of course, neither to the returning officer personally nor to the employing authority, but he or she is personally liable to account for them. It is essential that they be kept in a separate account distinguished from all other funds held for any other purpose.

Opinion varies as to whether you should have separate account for different kinds of elections. This has advantages, but the purity of separation is difficult to maintain when polls are so frequently combined nowadays (see chapter 24). It is not unlawful or inappropriate to maintain only one election account, but equally bank costs or bank interest may then have to be apportioned, with similar difficulty. Ultimately this is a personal responsibility and decision and you must make a pragmatic choice. A possible compromise might be to keep separate Home Office or other recharged elections from ones paid by your employing authority, but there is no final tidy solution.

The Home Office will advance a substantial sum by way of advance to most operating costs at the start of a Parliamentary or European election process for which they ultimately pay the costs (though not general office overheads outside permitted headings). If that money is not held for long periods, it will not be expected to earn interest, but any so received is liable to be accounted for.

Parliamentary accounts have to be submitted to the Home office for inspection - there is a special unit, currently based in Liverpool, who undertake this work. They often raise queries on various payments and their allocation within the accounts. Thus, for example, if you seek to recover loss of hiring fees for a public hall being used for the count, you can expect plenty of questions about how you assess loss of bar takings. To be fair, following the European Parliamentary election of 1999 more guidance has been agreed between the Home Office and SOLACE/AEA on what is chargeable and what is unacceptable. Nevertheless, preparation and final acceptance of the accounts is never a rapid process; it can run into months, and often years.

Free banking for such occasions may well not be available today: such costs must be obtained from the employing authority if not able to be set against interest received, as usually it cannot be recovered by recharge. Today's rules mean that returning officers will expect to have to produce appropriate documentation to open accounts. A good way of styling them is to combine your own or your authority's or constituency's name with "election account", so that its purpose is plain to see and mistakes are less likely to occur.

Obviously the accounts you hold are not part of your authority's resources either, but it is good practice to include them in the authority's general audit plan, to guard against problems and to underline a feeling of transparency about how you handle, and account for, large sums of what is still public money. Remember too the "accountability of officers" provisions of s 115 of the Local Government Act 1972.

CHAPTER 23
LOCAL ELECTION EXPERIMENTS - PILOTS

The Representation of the People Act 2000 made provision for pilot schemes for local elections. This followed the publication on 19 October 1999 of the report of Home Office Minister Mr George Howarth MP's Working Party on Electoral Procedures, and the growing recognition (strongly endorsed, it must be said, by SOLACE) that the existing law was urgently in need of reform, both in order to encourage more electors to vote and also from a procedural point of view.

Pilot schemes, as they are called, apply only to local government elections (which does include parishes and communities – see s 17 (2) of the 2000 Act and s 203 (1) of the RPA 1983). Authorities must apply to the Secretary of State in respect of "particular local government elections" which in practice means main elections on the first Thursday in May (whether elections by thirds or whole council elections).

Section 11 of the 2000 Act gives the Secretary of State power by order to modify election procedures to accommodate pilots in whatever form he is prepared to sanction them.

Home Office Circular RPA 433 dated 21 June 2000 referred to the 38 electoral pilot schemes which 32 authorities ran for their May 2000 elections. Results varied - all postal voting brought significant improvements in turnout figures, voting at weekends appeared to have little effect. For an analysis of these first round of pilots see the LGA report written by Professors Rallings and Thrasher of Plymouth University, October 2000. Applications for May 2001 were also sought (and 4 schemes have been approved), though it was made clear that pilots would have to be cancelled if a General Election were called for the first Thursday in May 2001 as pilot procedures are not compatible in law with Parliamentary elections as combined polls. Not only must the latter obviously all be held on an equivalent basis, but it would anyway invalidate the purposes of a pilot if the effect of the experimental procedures on turnout and general electoral efficacy could not be observed in relative isolation from other factors.

It is likely that further pilot schemes will be approved ahead of likely wider electoral reform in the next few years. This is likely to be an issue for the newly created Electoral Commission established under the Political Parties, Elections and Referendums Act 2000.

As the work of the Electoral Commission develops, it will no doubt begin to change the climate within which best practice is established and, perhaps, take over some of the advice areas hitherto covered by aspects of traditional Home Office RPA Circulars.

For further discussion of pilots and the Electoral Commission see "*Waiting at the Bus Stop of ... Electoral Reform*" by David Monks, *Journal of Local Government Law*, Issue 5, August 2000, pp 105-110.

CHAPTER 24

COMBINED ELECTIONS

With so many kinds of elections the likelihood of overlapping processes, especially taking into account local by-elections, has markedly increased in recent years. Increasingly general elections have been combined with other main elections, as for example May 1979 and May 1997: the parish and community council elections due in May 1979 were statutorily postponed for a month. But largely because of local by-elections, and the pressure from local parties to use the first Thursday in May, triple election commitments are now not uncommon.

Combining elections is now primarily the subject of ss 15 – 17 of the RPA 1985. Under s 15 where either a Parliamentary or European election falls on the same day as an "ordinary local government election", or a Parliamentary and European so come together, " they shall be taken together". An "ordinary local government election" includes parishes and communities: s 203 (1) of the RPA 1983. (References to the European "Assembly" in ss 15 and 16 (as printed in Schofield) is an oversight as the term "European Parliament" is now statutory – see s 3 (1) of the European Communities (Amendment) Act 1986).

Election polls for related areas not definitely required to be taken together (for example a district council by-election in England falling on the day of the main county elections or a county by-election) "may nevertheless be so taken if the returning officer for each election thinks fit": s 15 (2), i.e. there may be more than returning officer involved.

A general election will, however, result in parish and community elections being postponed, as happened first in 1979, but this is now provided for generally by s 16 of the RPA 1985. (Section 16 also provides similarly for European main elections, but as they are held in June at present such a clash is currently unlikely. Similarly in Wales community council elections were postponed by the National Assembly for Wales (Day of First Ordinary Election) (Postponement of Community Councils Elections etc.) Order 1999, SI No 722.)

Finally s 17, which substituted s 36 (3) of the RPA 1983, then provides that the main district council and parish elections, or such by-elections shall be taken together, and allows regulations to provide for the procedural differences accordingly required. Section 36 (3) of the RPA 1985 has since been further amended to remove the references to Welsh district and community councils: see sch 18 to the Local Government (Wales) Act 1994.

What sort of matters does "taking together" involve? The principle issues surround poll cards, public notices, whether or not to use one ballot box (or if a busy station requires more than one box, whether votes for different elections are put into the same box), and at the counts how different votes are separated, ballot box totals verified, and so on.

Such detailed rules cannot be summarised here, but need to be carefully checked at the start of a potential combined election process. Clearly with the advent of the Welsh and London Assemblies, and local referendums for elected mayors, the permutations are much more complex than a few years ago. A provision particularly to note is reg 61(3)(b) of the RPR 2001 SI No 341, on dealing with absent votes for parts of Parliamentary constituencies coming under different council areas, and the duty of a registration officer for any part of such a constituency who is not the acting returning office for that constituency to forward the lists of successful absent vote applications to the acting returning officer.

Reg 65 of the RPR 2001 SI No 341 allows the issue and receipt of postal votes to be handled together if the respective returning officers at combined elections agree to do so. Regs 97 and 98 of the RPR 1986 prescribe who is to be the returning officer for the functions which reg 98 prescribes. The decision is one for local decision, but Home Office Circular RPA 304 issued on 9 January 1987, which dealt extensively with combined elections, recommends that "unless it is clearly impracticable to do so" (para 26), issue and receipt should normally be combined "to prevent users being confused by the receipt of separate sets of documents for different elections held on the same day".

For provisions relating to the combination of polls in Wales between Assembly and local government elections, see para 14 of, and sch 4 to, the National Assembly for Wales (Representation of the People) Order 1999, SI No 450. Sch 4 provides extensive modifications in relation to both county or county borough elections and community council elections.

For the requirement to combine polls for electoral mayor referendums, see K in chapter 3.

CHAPTER 25

CHANGES OF AREAS

The law on changing areas is quite complex, and keeping up to date with boundary issues of various kinds easily becomes a treadmill. The provisions have inevitable implications for election law as such: they are not central to this book, but an outline of the main areas may be helpful. The key theme running through all this work is one of numerical equality to make votes of equal weight - thus Parliamentary constituencies are reviewed to reach an average figure, often difficult with the easy movement of population in the United Kingdom - e.g. considerable exodus from inner city areas in recent years and growth of new towns such as Milton Keynes. That "Parliamentary quotient" is at present just under 70,000 electors.

A. PARLIAMENTARY CONSTITUENCIES

Parliamentary constituency boundaries are ultimately fixed by statutory instrument approved by Parliament on the recommendations of the Secretary of State. Those recommendations in turn are formed following a statutory procedure including a public hearing process, known as a "local inquiry".

Section 2 of the Parliamentary Constituencies Act 1986 established separate Boundary Commissions for England and Wales. (The 1986 Act was supplemented by the Boundary Commissions Act 1992.) The Electoral Commission and equivalent Boundary Committees replaced those Commissions under the Political Parties, Elections and Referendums Act 2000. (See generally on the 2000 Act Home Office Circular 5/2001 dated 7 February 2001.)

A local inquiry into Commission proposals must be held under s 6 (2) of the 1986 Act if a constituent area local authority, or at least a hundred electors in the affected constituency, object to proposals which the commission publish for change. Those proposals will be made every 8 – 12 years, and cannot come into effect until the following general election: see s 4 (6) of the 1986 Act. The rules as to how seats are to be redistributed are contained in sch 2 (as amended) to the 1986 Act.

Parliamentary constituencies are the building blocks for both European Parliamentary regions and Welsh Assembly regions: see sch 2 to the European Parliamentary Elections Act 1978 (as inserted by sch 1 to the

European Parliamentary Elections Act 1999); and sch 1 to the Government of Wales Act 1998.

B. LOCAL GOVERNMENT AREAS
The Local Government Act 1992 established the Local Government Commission for England; ss 13 –15 established the procedure and requirements for reviews. That Act replaced the previous Local Government Boundary Commission, but the 1992 Commission has itself now been replaced in turn by the Electoral Commission established by the Political Parties, Elections and Referendums Act 2000. Section 13 of the 1992 Act has been amended accordingly, but this is in relation to the overseeing Commission rather than to the review procedure itself.

When local government area changes are made, a wide variety of other matters need to be addressed. All sorts of things need to be similarly adapted to the new boundaries. They are effected partly by the principal statutory instrument making the boundary alterations themselves, and partly by the general Local Government Area Changes Regulations 1976, SI No 246, amended by SI 1978 No 247.

For structural changes under s 17 of the Local Government Act 1992 the 1976 Regulations do not apply, and the requirements are instead effected by the Local Government Changes for England Regulations 1994, SI No 867 (see para 1(3)), as augmented by SIs 1995 Nos 590, 1055 and 1748.

The Local Government Act 1997 had also created a Local Government Boundary Commission for Wales, and prescribed a boundary review procedure in ss 53 – 59. Though necessarily somewhat amended, these provisions continue following the Welsh reorganisation under the Local Government (Wales) Act 1994. Under s 20 of the Political Parties, Elections and Referendums Act 2000 the functions of the Welsh Boundary Commission are transferred to the Electoral Commission and its Boundary Committee for Wales.

C. LOCAL GOVERNMENT ELECTORAL BOUNDARIES
Within local government areas, electoral area boundaries – wards or, in the case of counties, electoral divisions – are reviewed and modified in England under the procedures of the amended Local Government Act 1992 as noted in B above.

The principal review provision are, as for B, above, set out in ss 13 – 15 of the 1992 Act, and we need not refer to them in detail there. The final results of a review, as for Parliamentary constituencies, are set out in a statutory instrument approved by Parliament on the recommendations in turn of the Electoral Commission via its Boundary Committee for England and, if so accepted, by the Secretary of State. They will ordinarily come into effect for the next ordinary or "main" local government elections for the area concerned.

The "rules to be observed in considering electoral arrangements" were prescribed by sch 11 to the Local Government Act 1972, as now amended.

For Wales the approach had necessarily to be modified when unitary local government was introduced by the Local Government (Wales) Act 1994. Sections 6 and 7 of the 1994 Act substituted s 64 of the Local Government Act 1972 and amended sch 11.

D. PARISHES AND COMMUNITIES
The Local Government and Rating Act 1997 provided a new code of powers for district and unitary local authorities in England to review their areas and, under s 9, to make recommendations to the Secretary of State for the creation, abolition or amendment of parishes. The review procedure is provided by s 10 and the sections which follow. Section 11 of the 1997 Act allows 250 local government electors from an unparished area (or 10% of the electors, whichever number is greater) to petition "a district council or unitary county council" for the establishment of a parish council for that area. Reviews to be conducted by the former Local Government Commission are now the province of the new Electoral Commission following the passing of the Political Parties, Elections and Referendums Act 2000.

In Wales the previous provisions of the Local Government 1972 (ss 27 – 29) were substituted and augmented by ss 8 – 12 of the Local Government (Wales) Act 1994. There is no direct Welsh equivalent of s 19 of the Local Government and Rating Act 1997, allowing the Secretary of State to instruct the Local Government Commission (now the Electoral Commission) to conduct a parish review.

APPENDIX 1
FURTHER READING AND SOURCES OF INFORMATION

Surprisingly, for such an extensive area of local government work, there are comparatively few books written upon this subject. The two standard textbooks appear in encyclopaedia form and are widely consulted by all electoral practitioners; they also figure in all law libraries. Parker's appears in one volume and sets out to concentrate upon Parliamentary elections, although there are elements of cross-referencing to local elections. It is published by Butterworths; their address is referred to below. The other encyclopaedia is Schofield which now appears in 4 volumes. Originally designed to deal with local elections, it also contains material relevant to Parliamentary elections. It is published by Shaw and Sons who also produce electoral stationery used by practitioners – e.g. nomination forms, guidance as to doubtful papers, etc.

SOLACE and the AEA co-operated during 1998/99 to produce much training material for the European Parliamentary election of June 1999. This was facilitated by a Home Office grant and text books on legislation as well as training manuals were printed. There was also an evaluation report on the European election prepared by the University of Swansea. Some of this material is still available from SOLACE and/or TADS, the original printers.

The AEA as the main electoral administrator organisation produce a manual of good practice with up-to-date notes. They also run training programmes and seminars – as does SOLACE, the latter for both newly appointed and experienced returning officers; written material is always distributed at these events.

Prior to each Parliamentary election the Home Office produce a guidance manual for acting returning officers – it deals with such matters as expenses, nomination of candidates, the count, etc.

Although only very recently established, it would be anticipated that the Electoral Commission would produce information in the immediate future. Their address is given below.

There are a number of academics who write about elections, although they concentrate mainly on the political science aspects, particularly turnout levels and changing to proportional representation systems of elections. Amongst these are Professors Michael Rallings and Colin Thrasher (University of Plymouth), Professor Patrick Dunleavey (LSE), Dr Robin Butler (Nuffield College, Oxford) and Professor Robert Blackburn (Kings College London), to mention only a few. There are a number of academics abroad who write in a similar vein and their work can often be accessed via the Internet.

ADDRESSES

Parker's *Law and Conduct of Elections*
Butterworths
Halsbury House
35 Chancery Lane
London WC2A 1EL

Schofield's *Election Law*
Shaw & Sons
Shaway House
21 Bourne Park
Bourne Road
Crayford
Kent DA1 4BZ

SOLACE (Society of Local Authority Chief Executives & Senior Managers)
Hope House
45 Great Peter Street
London SW1P 3LT

(ALACE is the Association of Local Authority Chief Executives, a registered trade union)

AEA (Association of Electoral Administrators)
Council Offices
Foster Avenue
Beeston
Nottingham NG9 1AB

TADS
37 High Street
Shaftesbury
Dorset SP7 8JE

The Home Office
Constitutional & Community Policy Unit
50 Queen Anne's Gate
London SW1H 9AT

The Electoral Commission
Trevelyan House
Great Peter Street
London SW1P 2HW

Professors Michael Rallings & Colin Thrasher
University of Plymouth
Department of Politics
Drake's Circus
Plymouth PL4 8AA

Professor Patrick Dunleavey
London School of Economics & Political Science
25 Southampton Buildings
London WC2A 1PH

Professor Robert Hazel
Constitutional Unit
University College London
Gower Street
London WC1E 6BT

Dr Robin Butler
Nuffield College
New Road
Oxford OX1 1NF

Professor Robert Blackburn
Kings College London
Strand
London WC2 A 2LS

APPENDIX 2

PARLIAMENTARY ELECTION TIMETABLE

(EXAMPLE FOR 3 MAY 2001)

Proclamation summoning new Parliament/dissolution of old Parliament/Issue of writ	Thursday 5th April
Receipt of the writ	Friday 6th April
Notice of Election	Not later than 4pm on Tuesday 10th April
Delivery of nomination papers: Between the hours of 10am and 4pm commencing on	Wednesday 11th April
Last day for delivery of nomination papers	Not later than 4pm on Wednesday 18th April
Last day for withdrawals of candidature	Not later than 4pm on Wednesday 18th April
Last day for notice of appointment of election agents	Not later than 4pm on Wednesday 18th April
Making of objections to nomination papers between 10am and noon	Wednesday 18th April
Publish statement as to persons nominated (including Notice of Poll) and list of polling stations	Not later than 5pm on Wednesday 18th April
Last day for amendments to or cancellation of existing (long term) postal vote records	Not later than 5pm Wednesday 18th April
*Earliest possible first issue of postal ballot papers	Thursday 19th April
Last day for new postal or proxy applications and for amendments to or cancellation of existing (long term) proxy vote records	Not later than 5pm – Wednesday 25th April
*Last issue of postal ballot papers	Thursday 26th April
First day of requests to replace lost postal ballot papers	Monday 30th April
Last day for notice of appointment of counting agents and polling agents	Tuesday 1st May
Last day to issue replacement spoilt or lost postal ballot papers	Not later than 5pm on Wednesday 2nd May
Polling day 7am to 10pm	Thursday 3rd May
Last day for receipt of return of election expenses (assuming declaration of the result after midnight on polling day)	Friday 8th June

* At the discretion of the Acting Returning Officer

APPENDIX 3

COUNTY ELECTION TIMETABLE

COUNTY COUNCIL ELECTIONS – 3RD MAY 2001

TIMETABLE OF PROCEEDINGS

Publication of Notice of Election	Not later than Monday 26th March
Delivery of Nomination Papers	Not later than noon on Tuesday 3rd April
Publish statement as to Persons Nominated	Not later than noon on Thursday 5th April
Last day for withdrawals of candidature	Not later than noon on Friday 6th April
Last day for notice of appointment of election agents	Not later than noon on Friday 6th April
Last day for amendments to or cancellation of existing (long term) postal vote records	Not later than 5pm on Wednesday 18th April
*Earliest possible first issue of postal votes	Thursday 19th April
Publish Notice of Poll	Wednesday 25th April
Last day for new postal or proxy applications - and for amendments to or cancellation of existing (long term) proxy vote records	Not later than 5pm on Wednesday 25th April
Last day for notice of appointment of counting and polling agents	Not later than Thursday 26th April
*Last issue of postal votes	Thursday 26th April
First day of request to replace lost postal ballot papers	Monday 30th April
Last day to issue replacement spoilt or last postal ballot papers	Not later than 5pm on Wednesday 2nd May
Polling day (8am to 9pm)	Thursday 3rd May
Last day for receipt of return of election expenses (assuming declaration of the Result before midnight on polling day)	Thursday 7th June

* At the discretion of the Acting Returning Officer

APPENDIX 4

A MAP SHOWING THE 11 REGIONS FOR THE EUROPEAN ELECTIONS

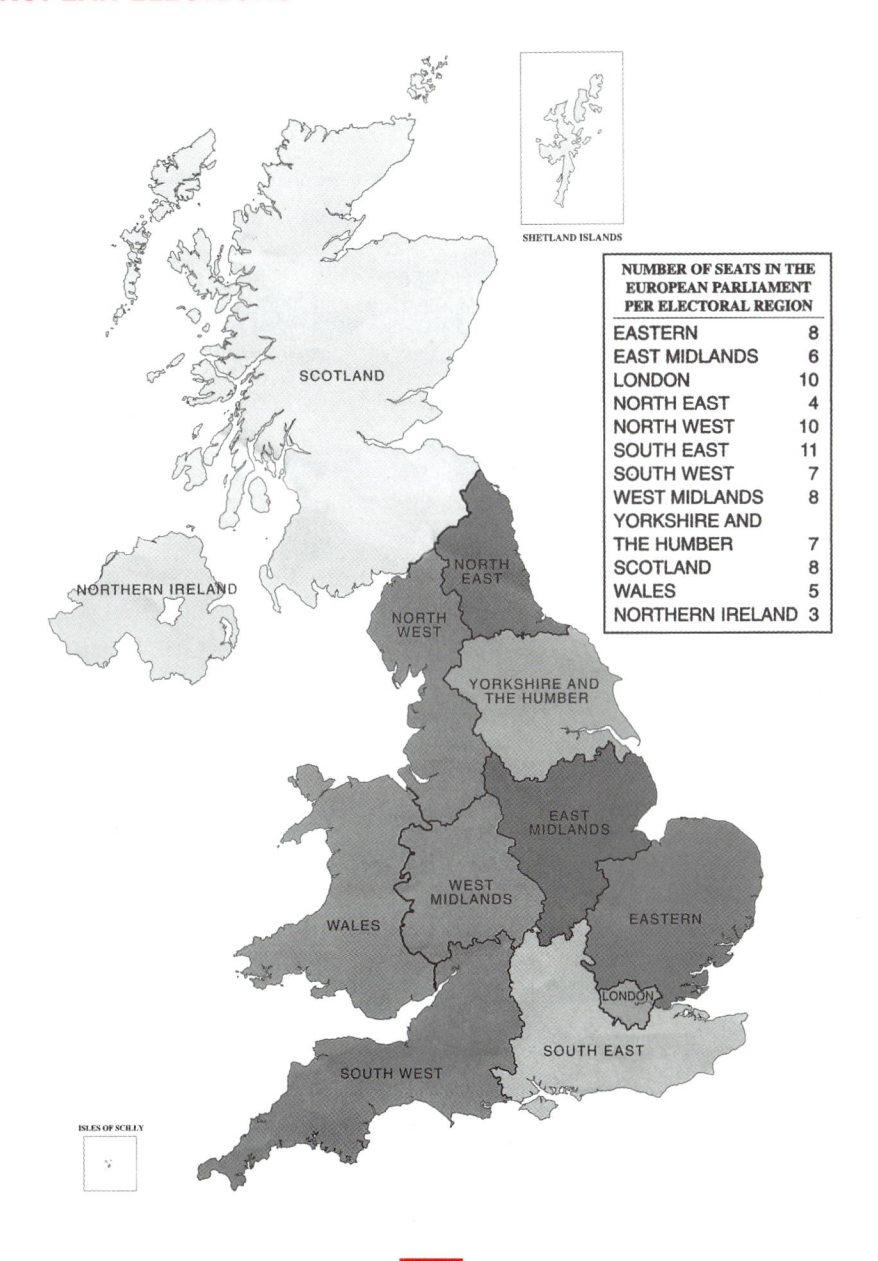

NUMBER OF SEATS IN THE EUROPEAN PARLIAMENT PER ELECTORAL REGION	
EASTERN	8
EAST MIDLANDS	6
LONDON	10
NORTH EAST	4
NORTH WEST	10
SOUTH EAST	11
SOUTH WEST	7
WEST MIDLANDS	8
YORKSHIRE AND THE HUMBER	7
SCOTLAND	8
WALES	5
NORTHERN IRELAND	3